Mamma Mia...
That's Life!

Mamma Mia... That's Life!

Valerie Barona

Matador
9 Priory Business Park,
Wistow Road, Kibworth Beauchamp,
Leicestershire. LE8 0RX
Tel: 0116 279 2299
Email: books@troubador.co.uk
Web: www.troubador.co.uk/matador
Twitter: @matadorbooks

ISBN 978 1785890 789

British Library Cataloguing in Publication Data.
A catalogue record for this book is available from the British Library.

Printed and bound in the UK by TJ International, Padstow, Cornwall
Typeset in 11pt Palatino by Troubador Publishing Ltd, Leicester, UK

Matador is an imprint of Troubador Publishing Ltd

For Alex and Elisa

Prologue

Lory looked in the rear mirror again and then checked the speedometer.

"No, non sto superando il limite di velocità," she said, *"Allora, vuol dire che ci stanno inseguendo davvero?"*

"What's the matter?" my sister asked.

"Nothing, it's okay." I tried to put Diane's mind at rest but she sensed that something was wrong.

Turning round, she saw the *Carabinieri* car at a distance.

"Are they following us?" she demanded.

"Of course not. Have they set their flashing blue light in action and waved us down to stop?" I wanted to make light of the matter but at the back of my mind I couldn't help but wonder whether it was a coincidence or not.

There were five of us in Lory's car and she'd noted that the police car had been behind us since leaving Sondrio.

"A Morbegno, giro a sinistra e andiamo al Dolce Forno," she said.

"What did she say?" Diane naturally expected a translation so I told her we were going to turn left at Morbegno and go to the *Dolce Forno Bar* for a drink.

From my position in the back, I could just see the wing mirror and as we went round the roundabout and took the exit on the left, so did the police car.

"Avevi ragione. Ci stanno seguendo sul serio," I joked and the others – except Diane – laughed, too. She was too busy craning her neck to see who was behind us.

"I have to get the flight home tomorrow," she said when she realised the police were still there.

"Don't worry, you will."

As Lory parked the car, the Italian police car stopped directly behind us. The seriousness of the situation hit us when one of the uniformed officers walked up to the car door and waited for Lory to open it, while the other stood a short distance away, watching us. Now what was going to happen…and more to the point, how would we explain the contents of the boot and the overflowing bags of brand new articles for the lucky dip and the lottery at our feet?

1

Villa Barona

Four years had passed since I boarded the plane at Gatwick Airport in July, 1977 with my fiancé to start a new life in his mountain village in northern Italy. After the initial shock of finding myself in a time warp where the middle-aged women scrubbed their clothes clean in a stone washing trough in the village square, and the old men still used a horse and cart to transport hay and logs from one place to another, I had to decide as to whether I could adapt to the ways of Piussogno.

Michele's decision to build a disco with his brother had prompted varying reactions from the locals but as they watched it materialise and some even ventured inside, they had to admit that it could do no harm. The 'Rendez Vous' was a family concern with relatives giving a hand. In fact, its popularity grew fast and furiously, especially as it was assigned a prize for being the very first disco in the Valtellina. Michele and Pietro had to go to Milan to collect it – fame, indeed.

Our wedding sealed the approval of the villagers and if they didn't agree with us moving out of the paternal home in preference for renting our own flat, the birth of our son, Alex restored our status.

Although our contract to stay in the *Gusmeroli's* flat was for two years, we were still living there three years later. I enjoyed Nanda's company and I knew I'd miss her two children popping up for *merenda* in the afternoon but now I longed for a place of our own. I was pregnant again and although sometimes tempted to return to Poole with Michele and Alex, after much deliberation and soul searching, I decided to make my home in Italy.

"I've just 'eard the piece of land by the side of the disco is up for sale," Michele told me. "It's a bit expensive but the Rendez Vous is doing well at the moment and we could afford it."

"Then buy it!" Impulsive as ever, I would have written a cheque for the land there and then.

Michele asked his friend who designed the disco to design our house and he referred us to his architect colleagues who, in turn, drew up the plans. Sitting in front of a desk in their office, they asked me how many square metres I wanted the rooms to be. How did I know?

"I want a reasonably small house: lounge, kitchen, bathroom, three bedrooms, with an en suite bathroom in the master bedroom and everything on one floor," I specified in my best Italian. I assumed that was explicit enough – it wasn't.

On our second visit, they showed me plans which looked so complicated that I understood less than before.

"Look, it's pointless talking to me about square metres because I don't know how big a room of 80 square metres is – I just want a house that's built on one floor." Michele detected the rising frustration in my voice and came to the rescue by asking them to build a model for me. That way I could see for myself the numerous sloping roofs and balconies which they claimed would make it unique. Obviously, they had not done business with an English female before who put practicality before design and who was also pregnant. In their opinion, my querulous behaviour was obviously attributed to my hormones running wild. However, when they presented me with the model, which Michele naturally had to pay for, I must confess that the modern design of the miniature house looked good and I gave the go-ahead.

Michele called the same builders who had built the disco and building began in April 1981. They finished it in July, just before the birth of Elisa and once again, we gave the villagers something to talk about. Every day I'd walk down with Alex to see the progress of the building work, stopping to speak to the locals on the way. Each one tried to glean a bit more information as to how the house would look when it was finished.

"How many rooms will there be?"

"Are you building it the English way?"

"Will you have tiles or carpet?" they asked in dialect.

I tried to answer as best I could – even though at times I was more concerned about the impending birth than the completion of our house which, in actual fact, resembled a villa more than an ordinary house. As the building progressed I began to panic. It didn't appear to be that small to me. Thank goodness I'd stressed the fact that I wanted a *small* house and not a *big* one. I'd have ended up with a hotel.

Built on slightly raised land, it stood out as a lone piece of futuristic architecture compared to the more usual square two-storey houses in the area. The high sloping roofs, giving intriguing angles, sheltered a number of balconies to the side and front of the house which offered breath-taking views of the majestic mountains encircling the valley with small villages snuggling between them. A shallow stream trickled lazily along the side of the house and lush woods stretched up as far as the eye could see behind it. Unfortunately, due to my pregnancy, I somehow didn't appreciate the idyllic setting of our first house together. I had other more urgent maternal priorities to think about. Michele, however, became more and more excited as he watched the progress and spent most of his time on the building site, helping out when he could. My father-in-law, Alberto sauntered down daily, puffing away on his non-filter cigarettes and nodded appraisingly at the latest developments.

I had specified, repeatedly, that I wanted everything on one floor but what I hadn't bargained for was a basement and a *mansarda* or attic, as well. To the builders and architects it was a bonus, to me it meant more cleaning. Three months later, Mum's arrival coincided with the builders putting the traditional branch in the chimney to show that they had finished their job and expected us to invite them for a celebratory meal. Michele and his brother, Pietro chose a restaurant by the lake. My mother-in-law, Carla, father-in-law, Alberto and sister-in-law, Mara joined us, too. Mum hardly had time to unpack before we were out again. Alex came with us, because in Italy, children are always included in such festivities. Everyone loved hearing him speak two languages and tongues would stop when Alex wanted to say something in English to his grandmother or me.

"Nanna, did you know that I've got a new toy car?" and as Mum answered someone asked what he had said.

"*Ho chiesto alla Nonna se sa che ho una macchina nuova per giocare,*" said Alex, totally unfazed by his ability to speak English and Italian.

He took great delight in explaining the names of the various cold meats to his English grandmother, served as *antipasto*. Occasionally he'd glance at *Papà* for reassurance and Michele would smile proudly saying: "*Sì, sì, è giusto.*" As if our son would get it wrong.

Mum still couldn't get used to how big the portions were. She had tried all the cold meats with accompanying pickles and had eaten her plate of pasta and was suitably full up. When the meat and vegetables were served she hadn't known whether to laugh or cry. After travelling all day, the thought of another course was almost too much for her. Alex loved meat and couldn't wait for his turn. As the waitress gave him a slice of roast beef and a piece of chicken, his smile widened and his fork hovered.

"*Grazie!*" he managed to say before devouring a generous helping of beef.

"We've got ice cream next, Nanna!" he added, excitedly, in between mouthfuls. Mum positively groaned.

"All I want is a cup of coffee and my bed," she whispered to me.

I knew just how she felt. When I first arrived in Italy, I remember being absolutely amazed at the amount of food Italians could consume for lunch and dinner. It wasn't that I'd been brought up on portion control but no way could my stomach cope with such large amounts of food. Another important factor I learnt was that you could never consider going to an Italian restaurant for a quick meal. There is a ritual about taking your time and enjoying the food and company; you could sit at a table for three to four hours without realising. Tonight, though with fatigue setting in, both Mum and I couldn't wait to leave.

*

Having decided on tiles for the floors of the entire house and not parquet or carpet, we had to choose the type of tile which was suitable for our *villa*. We wanted a warm coloured tile because winters here can be long and very cold.

We then had to choose a kitchen and a bathroom. I took Mum with me to the Furniture shop in the village to look at kitchens. Just for a change, the one that caught my eye was the most expensive kitchen on display – the rich chestnut coloured wooden cabinets captured my imagination and I could quite happily envisage myself cooking for the family – and, I must add that nearly forty years later it's still as good as new and I love it. Unfortunately, I can't say the same about cooking – I'm still waiting for my enthusiasm regarding culinary matters to materialise.

Next on the agenda were bathrooms and Michele and I went to showrooms to look at them together. We both liked one in a chocolate shade – coloured bathrooms being fashionable at the time – however, since then, my tastes have altered considerably and I'd change it tomorrow if I could. The bathroom had also been the cause of a *domestic*. I'd specifically asked for a large room because with two small children, I wanted enough space to move around but, I was told we only needed a small one because we'd only use it one at a time. Somehow, I found it difficult to imagine my two year old going in to wash on his own and likewise my four month old baby. As if that wasn't enough, I couldn't even have the toilet roll holder where I wanted it because it didn't *look right*.

"*Ma, sta meglio qua,*" the plumber, the tiler and company told me.

The fact that it involved swivelling around on the toilet seat to reach it just didn't come into it. *Bellezza* took priority over *praticità*. I fumed silently. My bathroom ended up smaller so that the master bedroom would be bigger. The fact that I didn't want a bigger bedroom wasn't even taken into consideration. Somehow my en suite bathroom didn't happen, either and both children had larger bedrooms than I considered necessary. The kitchen, on the other hand, remained a large room because I insisted on using it for meals, too. It had French windows which opened out on to the lawn in the back garden.

"I shall probably be spending nearly 50% of the day here in the kitchen, and I intend furnishing it exactly as I want to." I decided to speak my mind for once, before any forthcoming suggestions from various quarters over-ruled me.

The front door opened into a lounge with a small wall separating it from the corridor. Here, there was another dining area for guests then two steps led down to a smaller lounge where a fireplace had pride of place in the centre. I had been swayed in the end, by the romantic notion of cold, winter evenings curled up in front of a roaring fire. I had conveniently forgotten about the hard slog of chopping tree trunks into logs, stacking them ready for the winter and then carrying them up each day to light the fire. Not to mention the daily chore of cleaning the fireplace and sweeping out the ashes. I should have insisted on central heating only.

2

It's A Girl!

Our daughter, Elisa arrived on Friday, 24th July 1981 and coincided with the completion of *Villa Barona*, as I nicknamed our house. The previous consultant on the maternity ward had retired and his predecessor was not exactly the most sympathetic of people. He had a knack of reducing new mums to tears and his feral manner didn't endear him to the nursing staff. He marched down the corridor more like a general than a doctor and I could imagine him inspecting troops, instead of examining emotional females. Not surprisingly, I couldn't wait to go home.

During my week in hospital, Alex had become the talk of the village. At the tender age of twenty-eight months, he had made a name for himself as a simultaneous interpreter. He and Mum went to Giovanna's to do the shopping every morning. Mum would tell him what she needed to buy and he immediately translated into Italian. Within a few days, the shop was packed when they went – being English, Mum kept to a routine and always walked down at the same time – so word soon got around and they had an audience. I could imagine the scene, Mum with her list saying to Alex, who obviously felt very important and indispensable:

"Darling, we need some ham and some bacon." And Alex:

"*Vogliamo un etto di prosciutto e uno di pancetta, per favore.*"

"Then some milk and butter."

"*Poi, il latte e il burro, grazie.*"

Mum told me later how all conversation stopped when Giovanna served them. The villagers had never heard a child so young speaking two foreign languages. Alex also had to translate questions that the villagers wanted to ask Mum and, of course, the answers. He took everything in his stride, although becoming an older brother was a different matter altogether. According to him, the baby cried a lot and when she wasn't screeching, she was eating. On one of our first walks, Alex quite happily agreed to swap Elisa for a packet of sweets.

"*Ciao, Alex,*" said a lady coming out of the *bar*. "*Me la dai la tua sorellina? In cambio, io ti darò delle caramelle.*"

"*Sì, sì!*" And without hesitating, he took the woman's hand to lead her back inside before she changed her mind.

The main topic of conversation was how clever we'd been to have a boy and a girl which left me somewhat mystified. My own thoughts on the matter were how lucky we were to have two healthy children, never mind the gender. I was even more perplexed when several people said that I was fortunate to have a girl because

I'd have help when I was older. I hadn't realised that the object of parenthood was to guarantee *home-help* in later years. No way would I want my children to look after me when I was no longer self-sufficient.

We spent the following weeks organising Elisa's christening and choosing Godparents. We ordered a cake and enough rolls, cold meats and cheese in case guests decided to stay for the evening – which of course they did. Elisa wore the same christening gown as Alex and Don Giulio conducted the service in his usual affable way. The party afterwards was a success but then, when has an Italian party not been one? Italians certainly know how to have a good time.

The next date on the calendar was Mum's flight home and this time I found it exceptionally hard to say goodbye. However, with two small children to look after and *Villa Barona* near completion, there was no time for fretting.

We moved into our new home on 6th November 1981, ignoring the lingering smell of fresh paint and new wood. The whitewashed walls and large windows made the rooms bright and cosy. We'd spent a lot of time and energy furnishing it but it had been worth it. Sleep eluded me on the first night as a myriad of noises swept through the house. Outside, the stream bubbled over stones on its way to the river Adda, dogs barked, foxes screeched, while indoors, the pipes and radiators hissed and gurgled. As I wrestled with my insomnia, Michele, Alex and Elisa slept peacefully. Surprisingly enough, I couldn't appreciate the dawn bird song the following morning.

Unfortunately, it wasn't an isolated case and several more sleepless nights followed.

"Why can't I sleep?" I whinged to Michele over breakfast.

"Try 'aving a nap with the children in the afternoon," he volunteered.

"There's housework to do while the children have a nap," I sighed.

Michele decided it was probably to his advantage not to continue the conversation, realising that perhaps I still had to come to terms with a new baby and a new house, and my decision to live in Piussogno.

Being the first grandchildren in Michele's family, it was only normal for them to dote on Alex and Elisa, expecting to see them on a daily basis. Advice on how I should bring them up bounced off my ears and I smiled and thanked them, wondering for the umpteenth time whether I had made the right choice in making Piussogno my home. Since having children, I missed my own family more and to compensate for their absence I became a very English mum to Alex and Elisa which was difficult, living in a small Italian village.

"I'm going to speak English to our children," I told Michele when I fell pregnant with Alex. I'd already decided that the baby wouldn't be an only child, too.

"Yes, okay," Michele answered. "No problem."

But he was wrong: the language proved to be a problem. I didn't want to seem impolite in the presence of other people but from *day one* I spoke English to the children. It came naturally to me to speak in my mother tongue and I found it totally impossible to switch to Italian. This obviously caused a number of varied reactions from:

"The poor child won't be able to understand a word." To:

"How can the children learn to speak Italian and English? It just isn't fair to them." Or more to the point:

"What did you just say to them?"

I tried to answer as best as I could and explained apologetically, that I could only speak English to Alex and Elisa. Another important factor was that I wanted my family in England to be able to converse with them. Their English roots wouldn't lie dormant if I could help it. In fact, in next to no time, our children were bilingual talking in English to Mummy and *Italiano a Papà*.

Like English children, they also had a routine and I put them to bed early in the evening. This didn't go down well with visitors who chose to pop in after 8pm. Why put them to bed when they're still wide awake? Children should go to sleep when they're tired. How could the English be so strict? It just wasn't right.

*

Local parks with a playground still had to make their debut in Piussogno and surrounding villages, as did pavements. When we went for a walk, invariably it was a case of dodging the traffic. I had to keep to the grass verge and ignore motorists who took great delight in overtaking pedestrians at the last minute.

"Honestly, I never know whether I'm going to end up in Morbegno on the bonnet of a car, hanging onto the pushchair with one hand and holding on to Alex with the other. And why are cyclists such menaces? They always ride at least two abreast, if not more and although they dress like competitors in the Tour of Italy, their knowledge of the Highway-Code is sadly lacking."

"So, you went for a walk this afternoon," Michele nodded in sympathy, acknowledging the fact that I was having one of my *Baker Moments* (after my maiden name) as I called those days when nostalgia enveloped me and I longed to be back in my old home town where the children could play in Poole Park or go for a ride on the model train with Mum and feed the ducks.

3

Smoke Signals

Our life soon fell into a pattern: playing with the children, shopping, cooking, and cleaning. The disco, which Michele and his brother Pietro had opened at the end of 1977, continued to be a success and our weekends flew by in a flurry of colour and music. Another bonus was that with the Rendez Vous being next door, Michele didn't have far to go to work and Alex often went with him. Michele's father, Alberto, usually came down every day, puffing on his trademark non-filter cigarettes. One sunny afternoon, I walked down with the children and sat on some boulders nearby to watch as Michele stacked crates of bottles. Alberto arrived soon after and, wanting to speak to the children, put the half-smoked cigarette in the top pocket of his jacket. After a while, Alex started tugging at my sleeve:

"Look, Mummy, *Nonno's* smoking lots!"

"Yes, darling, I know." I continued amusing Elisa with her finger puppets.

"Mummy, *Nonno's* smoking lots and lots and lots and he hasn't got a cigarette in his mouth!"

I glanced towards Alberto and gasped. Smoke spiralled quietly out of his pocket into the air as he moved backwards and forwards lugging beer crates and somehow neither he nor Michele noticed the greyish puffs swirling above them. Jumping up, I sprinted to where the two men were working, shouting to Alberto to take out the offending cigarette butt before the jacket went up in flames. When he finally understood that it wasn't a replay of an earlier moment when I'd tried to explain my encounter with a pair of psycho-turkeys in the village, he quickly extracted the cigarette and winking at me, calmly placed it once more between his lips, inhaling deeply.

"Grazie," he said, *"di solito si spegne subito…chissà stavolta."* With a broad grin, he patted the smouldering hole in his jacket pocket and resumed his job in hand.

I couldn't help glaring at Michele as he took out a Marlboro and lit it. We'd had quite a few arguments over tobacco, especially after the birth of our two children but still he continued the habit I abhorred. It wasn't only him, though. I got the impression that the majority of Italians smoked.

"I'm sure they throw their dummies away and substitute them with cigarettes," I'd told Mum one day when she was visiting. "If I'd saved a one thousand *lira* note every time someone offered me a cigarette, I'd have been a millionaire by now."

I truly hoped my children wouldn't smoke when they were older.

"If you want to kill yourself, okay," I told Michele in a fit of anger one day, "but don't make our children passive smokers. Think of them and their health." He managed to look contrite for a while before lighting up again.

Despite their father's *nicotine vice*, Alex and Elisa grew into healthy Anglo-Italians that is until, my youngest, at 18 months old, developed a penchant for *espressos* and cigarettes.

"Feffè," Elisa would say, making a beeline for her father's coffee cup, knowing that he would let her drink the last sweet drops. Then, if Michele left his cigarette in an ashtray, Elisa would break a *toddler record* to pick it up between two cherubic fingers and put it to her lips, inhaling just like her father. The first time she did it, we were convinced she'd end up at A&E and we'd end up in court but, thankfully, there were no side effects. Unfortunately, it didn't turn out to be an isolated case and we didn't know whether to laugh or cry. She even managed a few puffs on the pipe I'd given Michele for his birthday when he inadvertently left it on the coffee table. I could imagine my mum's face when I gave her the latest update on her grandchildren:

"Alex is fine but this week Elisa's addicted to coffee and cigarettes and enjoys the odd pipe."

In the end, we decided to keep the ashtrays out of her reach and to pour milk into the coffee dregs. Whether the child psychology worked or she simply tired of the latest craze, we'll never know – suffice to say that she gave up *espressos* and cigarettes before she was out of nappies.

4

Sausages and Baked Beans

"You've got a letter." Michele came into the kitchen to find me. "And it's not from your mum."

"Really?" I had no idea who the sender could be.

"Well?" Now it was Michele's turn to be impatient.

"It's from a German lady in Morbegno inviting all foreigners in this area to meet up at Hotel Posta in Sondrio on 10th November. How did she know I'm English, living in Piussogno?"

"Word gets around, you know."

The phrase: *I heard it through the grapevine* just had to have its origins in Italy.

It was 1982, and apart from Kathy who worked in a travel agency in Morbegno, I hadn't met any other English people. Michele was only too happy for me to go and as Kathy had also received a letter, we naturally opted to go together.

That evening, thirty-five women turned up and between us there were fifteen nationalities. After a polite introduction to the foreigners present, Kathy and I gravitated towards the English. There were ten of us and as we chatted away about our new lives in the Valtellina, the succulent menu was ignored.

"What do you miss most about home?" Although some of us had already been living here for several years, we still referred to England as *home*.

"I really miss sausages and baked beans."

"Oh, I don't. I miss Marmite and gravy and custard and…"

"I could do with a boxful of Typhoo teabags and packets of self-raising flour. I always forget to add the yeast when I make a cake here. My dog is putting on weight – he's probably the only one who's happy with my attempts at cooking."

"Tell me about it! My mother-in-law is a great cook and I can't even boil an egg."

I could definitely identify with Gill.

"Yes, but there must be some things we don't miss."

Silence. No-one could think of anything but before depression set in with a vengeance, waitresses appeared with plates of roast beef which, unfortunately, wasn't the same as our idea of how roast beef should be prepared.

"Don't tell me this is how Italians think we eat roast beef!" Lisa was shocked. "Someone should explain that we eat it cooked – not raw." Everyone laughed.

Despite our differences regarding food, we had a great time that evening and promised to stay in touch. The Foreigners' Club proved to be a great success and a welcome outlet for sharing our 'missing home' grievances. Over the next few years, we met up on a regular basis, sharing our problems and coming home feeling much better. But, before we knew it, there were only four of us left. The rest of the English contingent, unable to adapt totally to the Italian way of life, had chosen to go back to England with or without their partners.

When one of the English group decided to go home to Devon, she asked me if I'd like to have her pool table. She and her husband had run two *bars* but I'd never actually seen the games room and automatically imagined it to be for children.

"Michele will have to come and fetch it with his lorry," she told me.

"How big is it?"

"It's a full size billiard table," she explained, patiently.

"How much are you selling it for?" I wasn't sure I wanted to know the answer.

"I'm giving it to you, otherwise it'll be thrown away," she smiled. "Oh and there's a matching cabinet to store the cues and it has a score board, too. It's all in pieces at the moment and will have to be put together."

The following weekend, Michele and I had quite a surprise when we came face to face with none other than a professional disassembled billiard table.

"I'm sure it's made of cherry wood," Michele said, gliding his hand over the dark shiny surface.

"Well, whatever it's made of, I could never have got all this into our car," I said as we loaded the large rectangular pieces onto the lorry. Having seen the exceptional condition it was in, Michele suggested a purchase price which was accepted appreciatively.

We stored it in the upstairs floor where it lay for several years until the sound of rodents' teeth during the early hours made us think that maybe it was time to call a technician to build it up again.

5

Only Italian, Please!

When Alex celebrated his third birthday, we had to think about sending him to *asilo,* (pre-school) the following September, in Cercino, the village above Piussogno. This proved yet another bone of contention between Michele and myself because in Italy, children attending first, middle and senior schools have lessons lasting half a day, and come home for lunch, whereas the children of pre-school age go all day. It was a contradiction in terms. I had expected Alex to go for a few hours in the morning as they did in England. The idea that I had to take him to catch the school bus at 8.30am and to fetch him again at 4pm didn't appeal to me.

"We're living in Italy," Michele told me quite adamantly, "and you 'ave to accept the Italian way of life."

"I may be living in Italy but I'm still very English," I countered.

I ignored comments from other mothers who assured me I'd enjoy having more time on my hands, meeting up for coffee with friends or going shopping. I wondered how they thought I would be socialising more when I still had a young daughter to look after. In the end, Michele and I came to an agreement: I would fetch Alex after lunch unless he asked me to stay all day.

The *asilo* had also served as a first school in the past and now, as well as being a pre-school, it also doubled as the doctor's surgery once a week. It was a large two-storey building on the outskirts of the village with a play area and lots of grass around it for the children to run about and shed any excess energy.

"We've got to buy you two black overalls to wear on top of your clothes so that you won't get too dirty, a pair of indoor shoes, a plastic cup for your toothbrush, a small hand towel, and a bib," I told Alex, ticking off the items.

"No bib!" Alex looked horrified at the idea. He didn't use a bib anymore and refused to even consider taking one.

"How about a serviette instead then?" He thought about it before nodding in agreement.

With his bag ready, he started counting the days until school began and it was only then that he realised he was leaving his baby sister behind and his Mummy and *Papà*. As we walked down to catch the school bus, he blinked back tears, saying that the sun was in his eyes.

"I'll fetch you after lunch," I promised him, as he climbed slowly into the *pulmino*. Going to fetch Alex meant I could see what the school was like inside and meet the two teachers. I wanted to see who the teachers were and which teaching techniques they used.

Not surprisingly, the small population of Piussogno and Cercino meant the number of children at *asilo* was minimal and when I arrived, I found them outside in the garden. Alex didn't even notice me as he played with his new friends.

The two young teachers, both local girls, came to greet me.

"Buongiorno! Venga a vedere la scuola." This was their first job and their enthusiasm was touching. One of them gave me a quick look around the school and explained briefly the curriculum. Then they introduced me to the cook and showed me a group of tiny beds in an anti-room for the children to have a little rest if they were tired. Giorgia told me that some of the younger ones were used to having a nap after lunch and asked to lie down. They told me that Alex had been shy at first but soon joined in the games. He had eaten his lunch and had sat quietly for a story. Watching him playing happily, I wondered whether I would be doing the right thing by bringing him home instead of letting him stay all day. When he finally spotted me, he waved and grinned and said goodbye to the children and the teachers.

As I had anticipated, Alex settled down with no problems. He loved it and after a few days, he asked me why he had to come home early.

"Mummy, please let me stay. I want to sleep in one of the little beds like my friends." Big brown eyes looked up at me, pleadingly and at that point, I decided to leave him until 4pm. Each day he'd come home with a picture he'd done or singing a song he'd learnt.

Just before school closed for the Christmas holidays, they put on a Nativity Play in the afternoon and invited parents and relatives to watch. Alex had a small part which he took very seriously and needed no prompting. When it was over, they sat round and sang a carol. Refreshments were then offered before the surprise appearance of Father Christmas. Each year, one of the fathers offered to dress up as *Babbo Natale* for the Christmas Show, and the children looked in awe as he walked through the door carrying a huge sack of presents which we, the parents, had already wrapped up. It was a magical moment as he took out the gifts and called the children one at a time to receive them. Impatient little fingers opened the parcels immediately and there was great interest among the mothers to see what I had chosen for Alex. My *Englishness* was still very much a novelty in these mountain villages.

Schools closed for a two-week break before school resumed after Alex's first term at *Asilo* and I enjoyed having my son home with me. He tended to speak to me more in Italian, though which I resented. I was desperately afraid he'd stop speaking English altogether but I needn't have worried. One day I made him cross, so with an arm around his sister's shoulders, he said: "Come on, Ellie, let's speak English so Mummy can't understand what we're saying!"

In his frustration, he'd completely forgotten that I was English. I continued dusting with a smile. Elisa was his shadow. He was her hero and she was going to make the most of having him around before school opened again.

*

For the next three years, Alex set off happily each day to go to *asilo*. When Elisa joined him, two years later, he was in his last year and was preparing for first school. Her first day was definitely more animated than Alex's. When she arrived, she decided that she didn't really want to stay and wanted to go home to Mummy. She tried opening the door but wasn't able to, so she did her best to climb up it, instead. Fortunately, the outburst didn't last long and she was soon playing with Alex and the other children.

There were only two occasions at *asilo* during his last year when Alex got off the school bus looking really miserable. Once because Silvia, a girl his age had been annoying him while he was trying to finish his drawing.

"Go away!" he said in English. Silvia slowly pulled herself up to her full height, and after looking Alex squarely in the eyes, she ran to the teacher saying:

"Alex just swore at me."

Although the teacher was shocked at this revelation, she still called Alex to her.

"You know we don't tolerate bad language here, don't you? If Silvia was annoying you, there's no need…"

Fighting back angry tears, he interrupted her explaining what had happened.

"But I didn't say a naughty word. I just said 'Go

away' – in English. I'm not allowed to swear anyway. Mummy says there are enough words in the dictionary without using bad ones."

Trying hard not to laugh, the teacher suggested he spoke Italian at school and English at home to avoid any further misunderstandings.

"All right," he sniffed, going back to finish his picture.

So absorbed was he, that he didn't realise anyone was watching him until he heard a voice.

"What are you drawing?" Alex turned round to find Silvia leaning over his shoulder. He still felt cross with her for getting him into trouble, but he couldn't keep a grudge for long and anyway, Silvia was his friend – most of the time.

"It's the beach in England where we go every summer. Do you like it? The sand really is this colour."

"Wow," Silvia was impressed. "Hey, come and see Alex's picture." She beckoned to a few other children.

"Is the sea really that blue?" asked one.

"Can you really see an island?" asked another.

"There aren't ships that big, are there?"

"*Maestra* Giorgia, come and see what Alex has done."

The teacher walked over to the group, happy to see that the disagreement had been forgotten and the children were friends again.

"Alex, would you like to tell us about your picture?"

Although not one to enjoy being in the limelight, he was always ready to talk about his second home, as he called England.

"This is Canford Cliffs where we go when Mummy finishes working – it's near Nanna's house. Sometimes we have lunch on the beach, too. I like making sandcastles and boats. And this island is the Isle of Wight – we can just see a bit of it. Very often we see big ferries going to Poole Quay."

"What's Poole Quay?" Greta asked.

"It's where lots of ships and boats go," Alex answered importantly.

"Poole is where Mummy was born, isn't Alex?" Elisa had joined the group, too and didn't want to be left out.

"That's right, Ellie."

"Do you eat pasta on the beach?" Enrico enjoyed his food and couldn't imagine a day out without a substantial meal.

Elisa laughed at the idea of sunbathers tucking into a plate of pasta at midday.

"No, of course we don't. We have ham rolls or sandwiches and crisps, don't we, Alex?" She looked at her brother for confirmation.

"You must get hungry," Enrico shook his head meaningfully.

"Nanna always gives us a big breakfast, so we don't want a big lunch," Alex explained.

"What do you have when you get up, biscuits and milk or a *brioche*?" Serena didn't often join in group discussions, preferring to watch and listen instead, but this time curiosity got the better of her.

"We have Cornflakes or Frosties with milk, a cup of tea, and a slice of toast. And sometimes, if I'm hungry, I have a second lot." Alex smiled at the shocked expressions of his friends.

"What, all that when you get up?"

It was a difficult concept for most of the children because going to bed late meant they slept on in the morning, giving them little or no time for breakfast.

The second time he got off the school bus looking extremely serious was when he was given the role of Peter Pan during Carnival time.

"I don't mind being Peter Pan, it's just that I don't want to wear a pair of green tights. I'm a *boy* not a girl!" Tears filled his eyes as he told me that the teachers just didn't understand. No way could he wear tights like Elisa. Nor had he bargained for his mother to take his teachers' side. In the end, we managed to find a pair of extremely thick, dark green tights which Elisa said she would never have worn because *'they were for boys'* (bless her) and the problem was resolved – or so I thought. Years later, Alex confessed that he'd never really forgiven me for making him wear tights. I explained that I hadn't been a parent for long and I was still working on it. My son was not amused.

On the day of the performance, parents and relatives turned up to watch the Carnival Show and we felt exceptionally proud of our very own Peter Pan. Come to think of it, his ready smile wasn't quite so genuine that day. Peter Pan will certainly live on in his memory!

I couldn't complain about their pre-school. Giorgia and Marina made sure they learnt the basic skills, teaching them in a way which made learning fun. They incorporated a lot of rhymes and songs into their curriculum and at the end of every term they put on a show which was very well performed. Sometimes, the children went for walks looking for chestnuts which the cook roasted for them. Several mothers asked me what I thought of *asilo* and the teachers and I told them quite truthfully that I couldn't have wished for nicer and more competent *maestre* and the location of the school was perfect for the children. My only criticism, if you could call it that, was the fact that these three to six year olds were away all day.

"*E…com'è l'asilo in Inghilterra?*" they asked me.

They wanted to know about such schools in England and I surprised them with my answer.

"*Ma, dai, vanno all'asilo per solo due ore e mezzo?*" They couldn't believe that children only went to play groups for two and a half hours a week. I explained that parents had the choice of sending their children all day to a private nursery if they wanted to, but, it made no impact. It was even worse when I broached the subject of first school.

"*E iniziano la scuola elementare a cinque anni?*" To hear that they started full-time education at five as opposed to the age of six in Italy was too much. How did the children manage to sit still at that young age? No, it just didn't seem right.

I diplomatically changed the subject.

6

Excitement in the Valley

Opening the shutters, I heard the sound of a helicopter nearby. So much for peace and quiet and a lie-in on a Saturday morning, I thought. When it's not the children waking up early, it's aircraft making a noise. Strangely enough, the throbbing continued to echo in the air. I went out into the back garden and looked up at the sky trying to follow the constant whirring of helicopter blades. The noise seemed to be coming from Cercino, the village directly above us.

"I wonder what's going on?" I said to Michele, who like me was craning his neck trying to get a glimpse of the helicopter.

"Per'aps they are taking up 'eavy equipment because someone is building a chalet up the mountain," Michele suggested.

"I don't think so because it sounds as if the helicopter is just hovering instead of going backwards and forwards. Almost as if it's looking for something," I added, certain that there had to be a more exciting reason for this flurry of activity.

"I can't say life's dull in this village," I laughed, straining to see what the aircraft was doing. Michele and I continued watching the sky, the incessant droning increasing and decreasing in volume until raised voices from our two young children indoors brought me back to the present and I didn't have any more time for daydreaming. The incessant whirring continued all morning and Alex popped outside every so often hoping to catch sight of the helicopter with Elisa toddling behind him.

"You'll never guess what 'appened," Michele could hardly contain his excitement.

I stopped feeding our 15 month old daughter and looked up, waiting for him to enlighten me.

"I 'eard it at the *bar* – everyone's talking about it. You remember the kidnapping they've been talking about on the news? She was kidnapped in May from 'er house on Lake Como …"

"Gaby Kiss Maerth?"

"Yes, 'er. The 'elicopter we 'eard this morning was looking for 'er and they found 'er."

"What? She was kidnapped and kept here at Cercino?" I couldn't believe it.

"No. She was kept in a place above Traona," he explained. "That's why we couldn't see the 'elicopter."

For once, I was speechless. My weekly letter to Mum would be infinitely more interesting than usual. So far 1982 could not be described as boring: to date my daughter had celebrated her first birthday in Poole and had taken her first steps on British soil and this was a fortnight after the Italian football team won the World Cup in July; my son had started pre-school in September, which was the same month I'd joined the Foreigners' Club; and now a kidnapping, which we'd been following closely on the news, had taken place nearby and it was still only 1st October.

Listening to the news that evening, we learnt that Gaby Kiss Maerth had been kept a prisoner for 148 days in a 'cellar' near Traona. A ransom had been paid, apparently, but the exact amount had not been stated. The 18 year old girl had been released earlier and was in reasonably good health. Michele and I looked at each other.

"The Valtellina is certainly on the map now," I said.

For the following days, newspapers and the media talked of nothing else. The kidnappers happened to be local people and the villagers took great delight in adding extra bits of personal information to whoever was listening. My daily shopping trips naturally took longer than usual and Michele spent more time at the *bar* discussing various aspects of the abduction. As the gossip mill churned out facts mingled with fiction, a story evolved about the kidnapped girl falling in love with one of her captors.

"E' vero, è tutto vero," the lady who had been embellishing the latest facts to a captive audience, nodded her head for emphasis.

'I'm sure it's true,' I thought to myself, trying not to smile. Italians certainly had a talent for drama. Their facial expressions and body language enhanced the urgency or importance of what they wanted to say at the time. They could make the most insignificant piece of information become a top secret scoop. Even my two children were showing the first signs of theatricals: their eyes became bigger and bigger as they gesticulated to emphasise what they were saying – which could be anything from wanting another biscuit, to not being responsible for breaking a toy – it was in their blood. On occasions, I found it extremely difficult not to laugh, but then who said being a parent is easy?

I did my best to teach Alex and Elisa to be good little people, explaining the difference between right and wrong, and taught them to be polite.

"You must always remember to say *please* and *thank you*," I told them.

"What happens if we forget?" Alex wanted to know.

"Nothing. But it's more polite if you remember to say those two magical words."

"We'll try and remember, won't we, Ellie?" Alex said.

Italians had a tendency to say: Give me… or I want… which grated on respectful English ears, especially mine.

After having the children, I realised I became less tolerant with some aspects of Italian life when I was tired or missed my family and it became more difficult for me to have *Baker Moments*, where pangs of nostalgia enveloped me, as the children grew older and sensed my mood. Sometimes I wished I could be walking along the beach at Canford Cliffs in Poole with my children looking for shells and pointing out ships on the horizon.

"Mummy, why aren't you smiling?" Alex looked into my face with worried dark eyes.

"It's all right, darling," I assured him. "I was just thinking about what I'm going to give you for dinner tonight."

"Oh," he grinned back, happy with my answer. Everyone knew how much I loved cooking.

Invariably on a Sunday afternoon, while Michele worked at the disco, I went to see Kathy at Morbegno. Alex and Elisa called her 'Auntie Kathy' and adopted her as one of the family. On fine afternoons, they played happily in the garden with Prince, her loveable Collie, while Kathy and I drank English tea and had a good old moan about anything and everything. We always felt much better afterwards and ended up laughing.

Very often, when we came back from Kathy's, we popped into the disco to see Michele. Music played an intrinsic part of our lives and the children loved going to the Rendez Vous. In fact, Elisa danced her first *lento* (slow dance) at the age of three. One Sunday afternoon, while I was talking to Michele's cousin, she let go of my hand and darted through a sea of legs until she reached the dance floor. A young boy got down on his knees and asked her if she wanted to dance with him.

"*Sì!*" she grinned, holding on to him and swaying to the rhythm.

"Well, would you believe it!" Michele and I were quite the proud parents.

Everyone clapped as the blonde toddler with big brown eyes smiled at her audience at the end of the song.

"Ha la musica nel sangue," Elisa's partner was suitably impressed by her musical ear – but I had no doubt that Alex and Elisa had music pulsing through their veins. They had grown up with the Rendez Vous and loved the psychedelic lighting and dynamic rhythm around them.

"Do you think all three year olds dance like that?" Michele asked me later.

"Only those whose father has a disco!" I answered.

7

Oh, Fiorentina!

Alarm bells should have rung years ago in Eastbourne when, as my fiancé, Michele chatted incessantly about his beloved football team, *Fiorentina*. Shopping in W H Smiths one afternoon, he stopped mesmerised in front of the stand of foreign newspapers.

"Nooo!" Sheer elation lit up his face as he picked up *La Gazzetta dello Sport*. Back in our flat, as he flicked through the pages looking for news about his team, nothing could distract him – least of all me. However, on my arrival in Italy, I found out that *Fiorentina* were *only just* in *la Serie A*, the Premier League. Their weekly performance on the field generally caused great suffering to their fans but fortunately, they seemed to rally during the last matches of the season to avoid relegation to *la Serie B*, the Second Division.

Whereas football matches are mainly played on Saturdays and televised in the UK, this was not the case here. Games took place on Sundays and they were not shown on TV. Depending on which channel you tuned into, a panel of ex-players, referees and journalists, commentated on all the games being played simultaneously, as opposed to actually watching them live. Occasionally, they showed shots of the public at the stadiums but Michele had to wait for the early evening sports programme to see the highlights of the matches. I found this most bizarre and told him so:

"Where's the fun in watching a player scoring a one-off Euro goal or a penalty kick being saved by the goalkeeper when the game's over? You can't tell me you enjoy just listening to comments on the game. It's ridiculous."

"*Cosa?* Can you move over a bit? I can't see." I did as I was told but not before a scantily dressed blonde waltzed on to the set holding a number 2 because a football team had scored a second goal.

"What the...why do you need a half-naked model to give the score? Aren't the commentators able to do it?" Michele didn't answer.

*

From the very beginning, I discovered a ritual to a Sunday afternoon. After lunch, Michele started commenting on the impending game: who *Fiorentina* were playing, where they were playing, who the referee was, and the line-up. Sorely tempted to say that I really couldn't care less, the look of nervous apprehension on his face stopped me and instead, I tried to make some intelligent remark regarding the possible final score. Whether he actually heard me or not was a different matter.

At 3pm, he'd religiously take his place on the sofa and wait for kick off or rather, wait for the commentator to announce the start of the game. What annoyed me most was the fact that the commentators only followed the team they supported and invariably were quite bigoted in their views regarding their opponents. They raised their voices angrily when their team didn't offer an hour and a half of nail-biting tension, arguing together making it impossible to understand a word. Still, this was Italian football and I had to accept it.

"What are you going to do now you have to work at the Rendez Vous on a Sunday afternoon?" I asked Michele a few days before the disco opened.

"Cosa?" Evidently, he hadn't thought about it. "I'll just 'ave to ask people I know to tell me the score."

If I thought that things would change now that Michele's dream of opening a disco had become reality, I couldn't have been more wrong. As all dedicated football fans will tell you, an unspoken pact between them is forged in times of dire necessity. Just before the start of the matches, a group of soccer mad followers left the dance floor and their partners and huddled together in a corner, heads bent over a small radio, a look of deep concentration on their faces as they tried desperately to follow the games above the throbbing of the music. If anyone needed Michele, they only had to look for what resembled a rugby scrum.

Whereas most football fans had the chance to applaud their team winning a match, Michele spent most of his time trying to justify his players' lack of initiative in scoring.

"I wish you supported *Juventus, Milan, Inter,* or *Roma.* At least you'd have the satisfaction of celebrating more often."

His reply was: *"Fiorentina* is *Fiorentina."*

*

Seeing Alex perched on his father's knee at only nine days old, watching *"90° Minuto"* the Sports programme giving the football results, I felt a pang of dejection: my son was destined to suffer like his father. Alex had been born healthy – but he was also born *Viola,* the nickname for *Fiorentina.* In fact, as he grew from a toddler to a little boy, invariably he ended up in tears on a Sunday when his favourite team lost. Once he started pre-school, he heard the other children discussing football and memorised their anthems. Michele was not impressed when Alex sang heartily: *"Juve, Juve, Juve!"*

"I'm glad you're behind the wheel," I teased, as the need to keep the car on the road stopped him from having an apoplectic fit.

"A quale squadra tieni?" Michele asked his son which team he supported. Looking crestfallen, Alex realised that he couldn't meddle with his father's sentiments where football was concerned.

"Ma Papà, è la Fiorentina!" he replied.

Peace reigned again. My poor son, brainwashed at four years old!

Very occasionally, a *Fiorentina* match would be televised and at these times Michele practically banned me from the living room – I had a habit of walking in front of the television just as one of the teams was about to score or I spoke at the wrong moment. I usually got the message, though and adjourned to the bedroom with a good book or I played with Elisa and left Alex and Michele to their *Happy Football Hour*. The pattern never changed. Before long, Michele started shouting at *his* players urging them to score. In his opinion, if they scored first it automatically gave them an incentive to win the match. The problem was being able to defend their goal area.

"Pass the ball, you idiot!" he'd growl, followed by a torrent of abuse when the player lost the ball. These outbursts had to be severely modified when Alex was old enough to repeat what was said.

"That's definitely a red card. Is the referee blind or what?" he'd splutter. At this point, he usually started pacing the room, gesticulating and waving his arms about, totally unaware of the fact that his son was two steps behind him copying his every move. When, occasionally, *Fiorentina* scored a goal, Michele jumped up, punching the air with his fist:

"*Sì, sì, sì!*" he cheered. This elated state soon become one of anxiety as his team then had to hold their lead. The second half of the game was always crucial: if they were losing, they had to draw, and if they were winning they had to defend their victory. Of course, if they could have heard Michele's *suggestions*, I'm sure they, in turn, would have been spurred on to win every game. As it was, I had to learn to live with a despondent fan hoping that the following week would prove to be a better game.

*

Michele came home one day with the news that *Fiorentina* were playing the following Sunday, against Como, at Como.

"Why don't we go?" he suggested.

"Why not?" I replied. Not exactly my idea of a fun day but it meant doing something and going somewhere.

We usually spent our weekends at the Rendez Vous, and had lost the habit of going out but Pietro assured Michele that he'd be quite able to cope without us for once. We decided to leave the children with my sister-in-law and her husband. Alex and Elisa happily agreed because they were always spoilt and usually ended up at a playground before having an ice cream.

We arrived at the stadium early to buy our tickets and also to avoid any fear of ending up together with the home supporters. I hadn't realised how near the stadium was to Lake Como. Several coaches from Florence had parked nearby and already an orderly line of *Fiorentina* fans waited for the gates to open. Como had been promoted into the *Serie A*, and their supporters proudly touted their blue scarves, flags and hats.

"I needn't have worried about being the only female," I whispered to Michele. Although this was 1984, I couldn't believe how many girls were there and not only those accompanying their boyfriends, but groups of them.

All of a sudden, the gates opened and we found ourselves being pushed towards a policeman, who wanted to see what my bag contained, and stewards who checked our tickets and showed us where to go. We took our seats behind a group of girls who quickly donned their purple scarves and started waving their banners. Before long the stadium was packed and a tremendous feeling of expectation filled the air. Adrenalin pumped through my body whether I liked it or not. At that moment, I was no longer an ordinary British subject – I was a *Fiorentina* fan.

A roar went up as the players ran out onto the field. The two captains shook hands, the referee blew his whistle and the ball shot up in the air in the direction of Como's goal. From then on, the atmosphere was electric. Supporters on both sides encouraged their team, singing their praises and chanting, but at the same time, they didn't accept mistakes and whistles were rife when the ball hit a goal post or a player missed the chance to score an easy goal. I learnt an entirely new vocabulary regarding football from the girls in front of me. They even shocked Michele. No way could we repeat what two of them wanted to do to *Passarella*, one of the *Fiorentina* players... I mean, he didn't intend kicking the ball straight to his opponent two minutes before the first half finished.

"We 'ave to score – at least one goal," Michele whispered to me, as the players took their places on the pitch for the second half. Once again, I was mesmerised by the sea of purple from the *Fiorentina* fans oscillating around me and shouts of:

"Dai, Socrates, passa."

"Passarella, fai un gol."

Most of the spectators were on their feet and we could feel the tension around us. Neither team had managed to score, despite numerous chances. Morale was running low and the language around me became less than eloquent. A supporter next to Michele looked as though he was going to burst into tears any moment. No matter how vigorously fans waved and shouted, no goal materialised. On the pitch, footballers shook their heads and tried desperately to find a way to fool their opponents but to no avail. The referee and linesmen alike ignored fouls and no amount of rolling around on the ground, faking a leg or knee injury would elicit a penalty kick.

After what seemed an eternity, the referee blew the final whistle and the players, with a brief acknowledgment to the crowds, took refuge in their changing rooms. A general feeling of despondency filled the air as we filed out. Nobody had expected a score of 0-0. Both Michele and I had hoped to have experienced the thrill of seeing *Fiorentina* score at least one goal. Driving home, conversation was minimal and for the first time ever, I had an insight into what Michele went through every week with his beloved team.

8

Hello, Hello!

After the heavy snow of winter, 1985 breezed into our lives with an air of expectation. Telecom announced the arrival of telephones in Piussogno and a month later, technicians started working. This was progress. I tried to be patient but the waiting period proved an ordeal: after the initial flurry of digging, laying cables and then resurfacing roads, nothing happened. Telephone wires lay dormant.

"What's happening?" I asked Michele.

"I don't know. Per'aps they 'ave to lay cables in Mantello as well."

Maybe, but why couldn't they just finish the job in hand instead of going on to the next village? I still had a lot to learn about life in the Valtellina. Patience is a virtue and the quicker I adopted the motto, the easier it would be for me. In the meantime, my phone had to have pride of place on a designer shelf and the two sons from the furniture shop in Piussogno came to take measurements and decide on the style. A week later they mounted their work of art.

"Well, what do you think?" They stood back admiring it.

"It's great, just great," I said, imagining the phone sitting there.

I think I felt more excited than the villagers when the technicians finally installed the telephone and tested it to make sure it functioned properly.

"I can't believe we've got a telephone in our house at last. Now Nanna and the rest of the family can ring us whenever they want to… and I won't have to pop to the disco to make phone calls anymore." I couldn't stop smiling.

"Can we phone Nanna to tell her?" Alex asked.

"We can try but there's no guarantee she'll be in."

The children took it in turns to dial the number and then we listened expectantly, our breathing almost inaudible above the soft intermittent dialling tone, until we heard a familiar voice answer: "Hello, 605159."

"Hello, Nanna. It's us, we wanted to tell you we've got our very own telephone…Mummy said you'd be out but…" I let the children have a quick word before having a chat myself.

"Mum, isn't it great? At last we've got a phone in the house." I hadn't realised just how much I'd missed not having one.

A few weeks later, I celebrated my thirtieth birthday and my family were able to ring me at home to wish me a happy birthday. For once, I didn't have a *Baker Moment,* with a lump in my throat, when I heard their voices. Having our very own telephone meant I could ring them anytime I felt nostalgic.

*

"Mummy, what's this?" Elisa asked one Saturday morning, pointing to the asterisk on the telephone.

"You have to press it to redial the last number," I explained and left it at that.

I finished making the beds then did the dusting – I was in housewife-mode, encouraged by the bright spring day outside. Walking back into the lounge, I suddenly became aware of a low murmur as if someone was talking quietly – and someone was. Sitting on the floor beside the telephone, my four year old daughter held the receiver tightly to her ear and whispered into the receiver. She jumped when she saw me and then smiled.

"I'm talking to Nanna," she said.

"You're what?" Taking the phone from her, I listened to the voice on the other end to make sure it was Mum before explaining what had happened.

"Oh, dear. I'm never out when I should be," Mum said and we had to laugh.

I suggested to Elisa that it would be better if she didn't touch the telephone or the asterisk again unless I was with her and she solemnly agreed.

"Good job Mum doesn't live in Australia," I told Michele later.

*

Our new piece of technology proved invaluable when a language school from Milan, *la Scuola 2F,* contacted me with the offer of a job to teach English to students and adults in the evenings.

"But how did they find me?"

"They probably looked the number up in the telephone directory." Michele couldn't understand why I found it so strange.

"Yes, but…"

"Certainly, everyone knows I'm married to an English girl and word gets around."

"I know that, too but I still can't get used to it. I mean, this language school is in Milan. How did they know that I, an English woman who teaches English, lives so many miles away in Piussogno on this telephone number?"

It had taken me several years to accept that the feeling of being constantly watched was really only a natural curiosity on the part of the locals. Now this oral network amazed me beyond words. Michele folded his sports paper and laid it on the table before continuing.

"They want an English teacher for this area. What do they do? They ask people if they know of anyone and your name comes up. They find the number in the directory and ring you. It's easy." He picked up his sports paper again and scrutinised news about the next *Fiorentina* match.

Explained like that it made sense but I still wasn't convinced. The next time they rang to confirm an English course, I asked them how they had found me. I could hardly believe my ears – it was just as Michele had said. I felt chuffed to have been singled out for the job but also apprehensive: no one had mentioned my qualifications.

"I wonder when someone will ask to see my teaching certificate," I said to Michele after the last phone call to give me the dates of the first course in Morbegno.

"They know you're a teacher, so why do they need to see a piece of paper?" Sometimes I forgot how *Italian* my husband could be.

"Because then they'll know I'm qualified to teach," I replied, none too sweetly but my words were lost as Bruce Springsteen belted out *Born in the USA* on the radio at that particular moment and Michele decided to do a duet with him.

In the end, the only credentials I had to give were my name and address. I fully expected to meet the organisers and undergo some sort of interview before the classes began but instead we made all the arrangements over the phone and the course material arrived by post. When I queried the fact that I had yet to have some physical contact with a representative of the *Scuola 2F,* the voice at the end of the phone assured me that someone would come to the first lesson in Morbegno. At that point, I could only presume that things were done differently here.

I arrived early for my very first teaching role in Italy and introduced myself to the man who had come along to open the place for us. It was an old building tucked away behind the shops but the room which would be the classroom for the next sixteen weeks was bright and spacious. Tables and chairs formed a semicircle and I had an antique mahogany desk with an old fashioned blackboard standing to one side. While we exchanged pleasantries, the door opened and I finally came face to face with *Mr Milano* as I'd nicknamed the voice on the phone. He exuded efficiency and elegance and gave me a contract to read before signing. I assumed he would stay and evaluate my teaching methods but instead he said a few words to greet the students when they had all taken their seats then he wished everyone a happy English course and left. I had no time to worry or panic – lesson one had to be a success. The next ninety minutes flew past.

The students were a mixture of ages: two 16 year olds went to school in Morbegno and wanted to improve their knowledge of the English language; others aged between twenty-five and fifty, wanted to learn enough to understand and be understood for holidays abroad. Their enthusiasm permeated the air at the end of the session when they each realised they could say:

"Hello, I'm *Mario*. I'm Italian. How are you?"

"I'm very well, thank you. And you?"

"I'm fine, thanks."

The students seemed to have enjoyed themselves, but I didn't really know whether their laughter was a tactic to alleviate the embarrassment of a total lack of comprehension or because they were a naturally happy group.

"Bye. See you next week," I said as they filed out at the end of the lesson.

"Cosa?" one of them asked, looking at me with a baffled expression.

"See you next week," I repeated slowly. "It means: *ci vediamo la prossima settimana."*

"Ho capito. Bye!*"* A chorus of 'Bye' followed them out of the door.

The man returned to lock up and I drove home.

"So, 'ow did it go?" Michele asked as I walked in.

"I think it went well. I'll find out next week if they all come for lesson two!"

I told him how *Mr Milano* had only stayed long enough to welcome the students without taking into consideration the necessity to check my teaching credentials.

"What's the problem? You are a teacher," Michele reasoned.

"I know and you know but *Mr Milano* doesn't know. He's never seen me teach," I argued.

"Look, did the students learn something and did they enjoy themselves?"

"Yes, I think so," I replied.

"Well, then. Don't worry."

I didn't. The following week all twelve students turned up and once again, the ninety minute lesson passed before we knew it. I discovered that three students actually lived in Mantello, the village next to Piussogno and another two knew Michele's family. I spent the next four months happily in the company of my students who gradually built up their basic knowledge of spoken English. They had a test half way through the course and then an exam on the last day. I naturally expected someone to come from Milan to hand out the exam papers and correct them, but no, it was left to me. I assumed I'd explained clearly and precisely the object of an end-of-course exam: principally, to see how much the students had actually learned – but I had to laugh when ten minutes later, the reigning silence gave way to a general murmur as they conferred on various aspects of English grammar.

"Puoi aiutarci con i numeri 14 e 17?" A couple of students asked me to help them with questions they had forgotten while others calmly opened their files to flick through the pages until they found what they were looking for. I realised the idea of cheating, in certain situations, came naturally and without guile to Italians. I smiled, remembering my theory exam for my driving licence seven years earlier. Expecting to find the same conditions for a public exam in England, I had watched incredulously as the instructor walked around the class pointing out errors, while the examiner calmly read his sports paper at the front of the room. Funnily enough, we all passed. Not surprisingly, all twelve students had excellent scores, too and, in true Italian style, we celebrated *la fine del corso d'inglese* in a local *pizzeria*.

So began my role as an English teacher for the *Scuola 2F*. I enjoyed meeting new people and found each course a veritable challenge. Taking evening classes meant Michele could look after Alex and Elisa. I loved being a mother but I also loved teaching.

One evening, a student told me he'd be absent for two lessons as he had to go away on business to England. The following week, he took out some photos to show me.

"I don't believe it. This is Poole. And look, this one's Sandbanks."

"Cosa? Come fai a conoscere questi posti?" He couldn't understand why I was so excited about the places he'd just been to.

"It's where I was born."

"Nooo!"

He explained that he'd gone to Sunseekers to discuss various aspects of interior design for boats. He enthused over Poole Quay, the town, the beaches; everything to him was *bellissimo!*

"Scusami se sono invadente, ma se sei di Poole, cosa fai qua a Piussogno?" Now it was his turn to be incredulous. A very good question, I thought: if I'm from Poole what am I doing here in Piussogno?

"Ask my husband," I replied.

*

After seven years, Michele and his brother decided to rent out the Rendez Vous. Although they were reluctant to do so, they had to admit that it was time for a change. Thanks to the disco, we had been able to afford a lovely house with a large garden for the children to play in but now they had to look for alternative jobs and opted to help their cousins Remo and Gianni in the building trade. The fact that I had just started English courses made the transition a little easier. Looking after the children and preparing lessons kept me busy and I didn't have time to worry about what the future held. Of course, I still dreamed of teaching in a school one day but until my teaching certificate was recognised in Italy, it wasn't going to happen.

Due to his new job, I had to get used to hearing a ream of dialect from people wanting to speak to Michele on the phone, regardless of whether I understood. Not wanting to seem totally incapable of giving a message to him, I took to asking for their number and suggesting Michele rang them if need be. Some phone calls were for me and were usually about English lessons. I'll never forget one from an engineer who did not join my rank of happy students. He introduced himself with his full title and in a rush of concise Italian went on to give me what I can only describe as his CV.

"I need to learn English in a month. It's very important for my job. I speak French and German but absolutely no English." Before I could reply he was talking again.

"I'm very, very busy and can only come once a week for an hour. Do you think you can do it?"

Was he joking? No, he wasn't. I answered in equally succinct Italian:

"If I had a magic wand, then yes, it would be possible. As it is, I can only rely on my teaching skills, and in my opinion it's unrealistic to think someone can learn a foreign language and be competent enough to speak it fluently in four hours."

"Are you telling me you can't do it?" he asked, angrily. I doubt if anyone before me had denied him anything.

"I'm saying that I think it's a physical impossibility."

"Goodbye." The communication was cut off abruptly.

"Goodbye to you," I murmured to myself.

*

"'Ello! Valerii? Is me. I come to you now?"

I loved hearing my students speak English to me over the phone – even if their grammar wasn't always correct. One of the most common questions was:

"When I learn to speak like you?"

I usually reminded them that I did have a thirty year start over them.

For the time being, my life revolved around English lessons, looking after the family and trying to adapt as best I could to an Anglo-Italian existence with a very much needed dose of English humour.

9

Don't Ask Mum!

If anyone had told me that village life with its laid back traditional ways would present numerous problems in my role as a mother, I would have laughed. I hadn't bargained for an on-going battle which involved overcoming discrepancies in everyday life regarding the upbringing of my children, namely: the language, food, and routine. The fact that I spoke English to my children – all the time – had caused a certain amount of disapproval in the beginning but I felt confident that it would soon be accepted and would no longer raise eyebrows. Unfortunately, the criticisms continued, but such comments fell on deaf ears. I was determined that Alex and Elisa would be able to communicate with their English relatives. Likewise, giving them a taste of English food encouraged a certain amount of head shaking and clucking.

Bedtime was another hurdle. As babies, I had had to contend with adults remarking on my strict regime but as the children got older, they realised that their friends didn't have to follow such a strict routine.

"Time for bed."

Alex and Elisa looked at each other and groaned.

"It's not fair," Alex said. "She sends us to bed when we're not tired and wakes us up when we're asleep."

Elisa nodded her head in agreement. It was a hard life having an English mum in an Italian mountain village.

"Nobody else goes to bed as early as us, you know," Alex was in argumentative mode. "I asked my friends," he added for emphasis.

"Bed!" I would not be moved.

Changing into their pyjamas, their stony expressions left me in no doubt about what they were thinking: their friends staying up to watch television. It just wasn't fair.

"Can I look at a book for a while?" Alex had no intention of going to sleep – yet.

"If you want to. I'll come and turn the light out when Elisa is settled."

Alex smiled to himself. That would give him plenty of time if Elisa went through her nightly routine of putting all her dolls and cuddly toys under the duvet before squeezing herself inbetween them.

Alex chose his favourite book and snuggled into bed. He'd asked Nanna if he could bring the Noddy books back with him and she'd been only too delighted to let him. At six years old, he had yet to learn to read Italian properly, let alone English, but he loved the illustrations of Enid Blyton's characters: Noddy was his favourite as was Big Ears and Mr Plod. He liked making up the stories himself, although I had read them to him so often that he knew them all off by heart.

"Time to switch out the light." My head loomed over him.

"Why is it always *time* to do something I don't want to do?"

"You'll understand when you're older," I answered, giving him a peck on the cheek.

Unlike his friends' mothers, Alex could never sway his mum. 'Must be cos she's English,' he thought to himself.

The *scuola elementare* at Piussogno presented me with another dilemma. The school had a total number of nine children, and one teacher who taught all five classes together. On the other hand, in the next village, at Mantello, a larger population meant more students and there were five separate classes each with their own teacher. Naturally, I wanted to send Alex there. However, if I chose the latter, then the school in Piussogno risked closing down. The parents held a meeting and I explained that I intended sending Alex to Mantello because I considered he would have a better chance of learning in a class with children his own age. I also let it be known that if the school didn't close down in the very near future it would have to eventually because there were so few births these days. I ignored criticisms regarding my lack of loyalty to Piussogno, arguing that I only wanted to give the best education to my children. I would not be moved and fortunately, Michele supported me in my decision. Alex, and later Elisa, made new friends and spent the next five years, very happily at school, at

Mantello. Just for the record, within a couple of years, the school in Piussogno closed down.

*

Whereas in the disco days my husband was always around, just before Alex started first school in September, Michele began working away in his 'new' job as a builder which meant that he wasn't at home to help with homework. Not that it worried me because I hadn't anticipated any more headaches.

Alex found himself in a class of eleven which to me was on a par with private education. The children called the teachers by their first name and it seemed very strange to me to hear them call out:

"*Maestra* Petra!" (teacher Petra)

We had a meeting with the teachers the first week and somehow, despite being the only foreigner present, I managed to be voted *Parent Rep.*

"Being class rep just involves attending a meeting with us every so often and highlighting any problems that arise. I'm sure you'll find these meetings very interesting as they will give you an insight as to what is going on in the school," the teacher explained to me, enthusiastically.

"I'm sure I will," I answered, weakly.

Although I had to admit that the staff impressed me with their enthusiasm which they inevitably transmitted to their students, I was sorry there was no lesson devoted to music and movement in the curriculum, especially for the first year, but at least they had singing lessons and were taught rhythm.

At the end of the first fortnight at school, Alex came home with a frown instead of his usual smile.

"That's the last time I'm asking you, Mummy to help me with my homework!" he announced, as we sat down for lunch.

"What's the matter?" I queried, quite concerned now.

"Well, you know *Maestra* Petra said we had to ask our parents to help us with our homework?" he waited for me to nod before continuing.

"You got it wrong and I was the only one who made a mistake!"

I felt like saying that he was the only one with an English mum, but I didn't.

Instead, I enquired as to what exactly I'd got wrong. He explained patiently that it was to do with animals and their young. Then I remembered. The teacher had given them the name of the adult and they had to write the equivalent for the baby:

e.g. *gatto – gattino, cane – cagnolino.*

When Alex came to *mucca*, I automatically said *mucchina*. Unfortunately, he hadn't insisted on *Papà* checking his work, having complete faith in his mother and this had been a big mistake …

At school that morning, when he read out his work, there had been great hilarity when he came to the *cow*. I had no idea that the word *calf,* in Italian changed completely. I had still to encounter: *vitello*. Alex looked at me accusingly.

"I'll never ask you to help me again. Never, never!" he said with feeling… and he was true to his word. From then on he always worked alone.

Not even the teacher could rectify the situation. Alex made it quite clear to her too, that he intended working at home alone. In future, I was only allowed to look through his exercise books to see what he was doing in class and nothing more. My lesson from that was: when in doubt – look it up in the dictionary.

*

In the first year at Mantello, Elisa found herself in a class of four and had practically one-to-one teaching.

"How did you like school?" I asked her after her first day.

"Mummy, I love it!" she smiled up at me. "And I told the children in my class I'm Anglo-Italian," she added, importantly.

I had told Alex and Elisa they were Anglo-Italian as soon as they were old enough to speak.

"What does that mean?" Elisa had asked at the time.

"It means you've got an English mother and an Italian father," I explained.

She came home very excited one day.

"I learnt a new song at school today, listen, it's like this:
*'Appy beerday, toh yo,
'Appy beerday, toh yo
'Appy beerday, toh yo
'Appy beerday, toh yo!"*

She sang it to the tune of Happy Birthday so I imagined it to be a variation of it.

"That's lovely," I told her. "It's just like the song we sing in English, isn't it?"

Her face broke into a disarming smile as she realised it was an Italian adaptation of the familiar song sung at birthdays.

Elisa's teacher was a supply teacher, so at the end of the first school year they said goodbye to her. For the following four years she had a new teacher and two new companions. Like her brother, she loved primary school. In a class of six, three boys and three girls, there was quite a family atmosphere. The teacher, with his grey hair and kindly manner, was more like a knowledgeable grandfather figure than a teacher. *Maestro* Matteo took great delight in giving his pupils a problem to solve over lunch. Sometimes it was to test maths, other times it dealt with social difficulties, often there was no straightforward answer but it made you think and discuss the various options. If I saw him in the playground during break time, on my way back from the shops, I'd often reproach him that mealtimes were becoming too academic for me and I invariably ended up with a headache. Laughing, he promised to send the children home with another even more complicated puzzle. His pupils adored him and it was reciprocal. When he organised the school trip, he invited parents to go along, too. We all accepted the invitation and spent an enjoyable day together, ending it at a local restaurant.

Maestro Matteo was due to retire when the class was in its fourth year but we managed to persuade him to wait until our children went to middle school. They all benefited from his style of teaching and many years later when Elisa attended senior school, she remembered his lessons. For her, and many other students, he will always be their *Maestro* Matteo.

Both Alex and Elisa had a very happy and privileged elementary education.

The only disagreements we had were when I didn't allow them to miss school during the grape harvest because I considered their education to be more important. I still let them help out once they'd finished their homework but for them, it wasn't the same thing.

"All the other children stay home to help with *vendemmia*," Alex told me and, as usual, Elisa nodded in agreement, but I was adamant.

"I'm pretty sure that you weren't the only two children at school today," I replied, trying not to smile.

"Non è giusto! Andiamo, Ellie." And with a great sense of unity, my children marched off together.

As well as giving them an English upbringing, I also hoped to instil in them a love of the place where I was born. I knew I'd reached my goal when they had to describe their *casa* at primary school and first Alex then Elisa had asked which home: the English one or the Italian one? Yes!

10

A Tutu and New Friends

When Elisa was six and started primary school, she decided she'd like to go to ballet lessons, so I asked Nanda and she told me about a good ballet school at Morbegno where Sofia had gone with her friend. I enrolled Elisa immediately and she couldn't wait to start. Chatting to her in English as I helped her change into her leotard, it came as no surprise to find another mother staring at me. It happened the next time, too, but I refused to speak Italian to my daughter.

"I'm sorry, if I'm staring, but it's so nice to listen to you," she said in perfect English.

"Oh, that's all right," I answered, completely taken aback. "No problem." Now I was the one staring.

We went for a coffee while the girls had their lesson and she introduced herself as Gaetana and explained why she spoke English so well.

"I met my husband, he's also Italian, in London and we lived there until our daughter, Luana was six. We decided to come back to Morbegno so that she could go to school here. You know, I really miss speaking English."

She turned out to be an affable rebel and we hit it off straightaway and so did the girls. She fulfilled the void that Kathy had left, a few years earlier, when she went back to the UK to live. I needed someone to speak to in English, someone who could identify with life in England and she understood perfectly. She talked me through various *Baker Moments* and together we laughed at certain episodes which incensed me at the time.

"Don't be silly," she'd say, "don't think about it. Come on, I have to go to the library." And off we'd go.

The girls enjoyed their ballet lessons and couldn't wait to perform at the annual ballet show held in a local theatre.

"I can't believe it's so late," I said to Michele when I told him it was going to start at 9pm. "I think it should be much earlier for the little ones like Elisa and Luana."

"Don't worry, they'll be too excited to feel tired." He was right. When Gaetana and I popped behind stage to make sure everything was under control before the curtain went up, they couldn't have been more awake. Leaving them happily chatting, we found our seats and settled down for the performance. As the little ones danced onto the stage, the audience 'oohed' and 'aahed' in unison. Some parents jumped up and waved, a few shouted out the names of their daughters, while others snapped away with their cameras.

"You couldn't do that in England," I whispered to Gaetana.

"No, you'd be asked, very politely, to be quiet," she replied.

This happened to be the first of many ballet shows held at Morbegno and at Sondrio. Both Elisa and Luana had main parts, often sharing the same role, as they got older. As well as ballet shows, they also took exams with the Royal Academy until it became too expensive for the ballet school. When possible, the teacher took her dancing pupils to Milan to see ballets such as Sleeping Beauty and The Nutcracker Suite. On one occasion, Elisa came home ecstatic to think she'd met and actually spoken to Carla Fracci, Italy's famous veteran ballerina. Unlike her idol, Elisa's dancing career ended in 1997, when she had to have a minor operation on her foot. From then on, she concentrated on disco dancing.

*

Another good friend who I saw on a regular basis was Emily. Whenever I had a free afternoon, I drove up the winding road to Cercino to see her. I enjoyed sitting outside in the shade talking about Poole and hearing her talk about her life in Spain. Whereas in England the topic of conversation always involved the weather, here, sooner or later, we found ourselves discussing food. Emily loved cooking and often explained a recipe to me but funnily enough, my dish never had the same look or taste as hers. Her *piatto forte* was naturally Paella. Alex and Elisa knew they would have a feast when she and her husband invited us for a meal. Their two children were a lot older than ours but the thought of good food outweighed the lack of playmates. I have to admit that even her picnics made history.

One Sunday, we arranged to go out for the day with them. We set off early and nine hours later, we were able to say that we had passed through four states – Livigno, Switzerland, Austria and Liechtenstein. Alex and Elisa couldn't wait to tell their teachers and school friends the next day but they'd also been suitably impressed by the picnic. Whereas we usually made do with a rug to sit on to eat our ham rolls, fruit and cold drinks with a flask of coffee, Emily and Nino suggested driving until we found a proper picnic area with trestle tables and benches to sit on. Emily then extracted a superb hamper containing a cold chicken, salad, pickles, cold meats, a selection of cheeses, fruit and an assortment of cakes. Not to mention the miniature cylinder gas stove used for camping that she and her husband brought out so we could drink an *espresso* afterwards. I shook my head in disbelief – no way could I compete with such efficiency. Alex and Elisa's expressions said it all.

*

Although I had been living in Piussogno for several years now and had become friends with other mothers, I still felt different and knew that the locals noted everything I did. The ten minute walk to Mantello, the next village which boasted a butcher, a baker, a bank, a chemist, a grocer, and a post office, could sometimes take well over an hour depending on who I met on route. I was and

67

would always be the *Inglesina* or the *English girl*. I learned in time that the villagers weren't being intrusive but were genuinely interested in what went on around them – especially if it had anything to do with the *Inglesina*.

11

A Baton and a Flashing Blue Light

"Do you know, I saw them again at the last minute coming back from Morbegno?"

"*Chi?*" Michele put his paper down.

"The *Polizia* ... or was it the *Carabinièri*? Anyway, they stopped the car in front of me."

For some unknown reason, I found it incredibly difficult to memorise the distinctive differences between the Italian Police forces. However, they all seemed to have one thing in common: a habit of hiding in discreet places by the roadside, stopping unfortunate motorists at random. They were prone to giving on the spot fines and no amount of wheedling or pleading would get them to change their minds.

Michele did his best to enlighten me and in time, I managed to define the three categories.

"I think I've got it: the *Carabinièri* are in charge of the general safety of the population and they have to make sure the public don't break the law; the *Polizia* defend the state and the people, preventing any illegal action or unlawful behaviour.

The *Finanza* are like our Inland Revenue and have to make sure every Italian respects the tax laws. They check lorries and their loads and fine any driver who doesn't have the necessary papers for transport and delivery. Right?"

"Sì, sì…è giusto. Brava!" Michele answered, suitably impressed.

A patrol had stopped me soon after I passed my driving test. Although I was the only vehicle on the road and was driving at a leisurely pace, I still only saw the giveaway *carabinièri* car at the last minute. The policeman strolled out in front of me and waved his baton while his colleague pointed his machine gun at me. A pacifist at heart, I wasn't used to being the target of firearms and ignoring the consequences, I bravely asked the policeman, resplendent in his uniform, to kindly point the gun in the opposite direction. Looking surprised, he lowered the gun.

"Grazie," I managed to say, realising just what I'd done. I mean, no-one dares to confront a police officer for fear of ending up with a hefty fine.

"Libretto e patente," asked the one holding the baton.

I obliged and handed over the log book and driving licence to be scrutinised.

"E' inglese?" It sounded more of an accusation than a question as he returned my papers.

"Sì, sì." And I'm proud of being English, I wanted to say.

"E… è un'insegnante?"

"Sì."

"Le piace qui?"

"Oh, sì, sì." I love living here so long as I'm not stopped by the police and fined, I was tempted to add.

They checked the road tax, insurance and tyres, then with a terse:*"Buongiorno,"* they let me go and waved down the next oncoming car.

I don't know why, but the police, regardless of category, always stopped me. At first, I felt proud to think that being a law abiding citizen, they could never find fault with either my driving skills or the car and therefore they couldn't fine me, but after a while, the novelty – if you can call it that – wore off. On one occasion, they asked me why I was wearing my seatbelt.

"Because it's dangerous to drive without it," I said, adding as an afterthought, "and it's illegal to drive without being strapped in in England."

"But you're in Italy," was the reply.

"Yes, but I'm English," I said, summoning all the self-control I possessed.

There was a great feeling of unity among drivers when police cars were found hidden in the most unexpected places. You always knew if there was one in the vicinity when a car flashed its headlights. The first time it happened to me, I thought it was someone I knew and wondered why they hadn't hooted. All was revealed when the inevitable baton was waved in my face about 400 metres down the road. The family were perplexed to think that so far I'd never actually been fined, even when one of the rear tyres was found to be bald; I was just given a warning and advised to stop at the nearest garage to get it changed. Thanking the policeman profusely, I breathed a sigh of relief and set off on my quest for a new tyre. Perhaps the helpless female role played an important part. Not being the *model type* and not possessing eyelashes long enough to flutter, I had to rely on other means, notably, my ability to act and so far it had worked.

I have to admit that once or twice I *might* have exceeded the speed limit and the police *may* have turned a blind eye at the emergency stop I carried out when the infamous baton appeared, but having checked my driving licence and noting that I was English, the conversation generally turned to my present situation and whether I enjoyed Italian food and living in the Valtellina.

Italian police don't give the impression of being the friendly, approachable type that we associate with the British Bobby. However, on the few occasions we have left the confines of the Valtellina and ventured farther afield, when needing directions, the urban police have always been very helpful and competent.

*

A memorable incident with the police force, was some years ago when I was taking my daughter and her friend to their dancing lesson in Morbegno. My mind must have been elsewhere because I was completely oblivious to the police patrol ahead and the policeman who was flagging me down with his baton. I saw him at the last minute and without thinking, waved to him and drove on. It was only when the girls started shouting in horror that reality sunk in. Looking in the rear mirror, I saw the policeman shaking his head in disbelief and gesturing.

"Mum, will they drive after you and fine you?" Elisa asked worriedly.

"*Ti arresteranno?*" her friend, Greta asked, hardly containing her excitement now that the initial shock had worn off.

"No, of course they won't arrest me," I assured them – but I confess to feeling apprehensive for the rest of the ride. I began to relax when we picked up Gaetana and her daughter and there was still no sign of flashing blue lights or police officers. While the girls had their ballet lesson, Gaetana and I went to our usual *bar* for a coffee. We were laughing over the incident when who should walk in but the two policemen.

"Oh, I don't believe it. They've found me."

"Don't be silly. They just want an *espresso*. Act normally." Gaetana always knew what to do.

"When have I ever acted normally?"

At this, we both had the giggles and the policemen glanced in our direction.

"With a bit of luck they won't recognise me." I tried desperately to regain my composure.

"Of course they won't. How could they? You were in the car when they tried to stop you."

In fact, they didn't and they left as soon as their coffee break was over.

"Another time, just remember to stop if a police officer waves you down," Gaetana suggested.

"Don't worry, I will."

Once again, we started laughing. The two of us together could never be serious for long. Not even over such a grave matter as eluding the Italian Police.

12

A Kilo of Patience

Eating is a serious business in Italy. The first thing I noticed on my arrival in Piussogno when I sat down to eat with Michele's family, were the two plates: a soup plate (used also for *pasta*) and a plate for the meat dish. I had been used to only one plate, for only one course but here it was very different. As the bells tolled midday, lunch had to be served. How I wanted to rebel and eat at 1pm.

"Most Italians only drink an *espresso* coffee for breakfast so certainly, they're 'ungry by 12 o'clock," Michele explained.

We always had a plate of *pasta* followed by meat, vegetables or salad and cheese then coffee brought the meal to an end. No wonder Italians needed a *siesta* afterwards. Having eaten such a heavy meal, no one could go straight back to work.

"Don't you have a cup of tea in the afternoon?" I'd queried during my initiation to Italian life.

"You only 'ave *merenda* – that's a drink with a biscuit or cake – if a visitor turns up," Michele said. "That's why we 'ave another big meal in the evening."

I groaned. With my culinary attributes – or lack of – I'd certainly chosen the right country to live in. Sometimes, I really had a craving for a plate of baked beans-on-toast.

One spring afternoon I saw Carla picking what I thought to be dandelions.

"What's she doing?" I asked Michele as we walked down to the disco to finish the cleaning after a busy weekend.

"We always eat the first dandelions with a boiled egg. Certainly, they're very good for you." I glanced at Michele to see whether he was teasing me. Unfortunately, he wasn't.

"What, you actually eat them?" I wasn't exactly looking forward to the evening meal.

"Well, not raw. You 'ave to boil them first."

"Oh, that makes all the difference, then." I wondered what other surprises were in store for me. Having accepted the fact that rabbits and chickens were kept not as pets but as part of a variant to the menu, I still shuddered when I saw the skinned bodies lying over the garden railings ready for the pot.

Although this has never been one of my favourite dishes, if the French can eat snails, then I can eat dandelions and their leaves…

*

"*Mamma's* cooking *Pizzoccheri* today and we're invited," Michele announced a couple of days after we'd moved into our new house.

"Oh," I tried to sound enthusiastic but I found it a very filling dish and not one of my favourites. My mind wandered back to my debut of Italian meals and the day my mother-in-law had told us that she intended making *Pizzoccheri* for lunch.

"What is it? *Pasta* by any chance?" I'd asked with tongue firmly in cheek.

"The *Valtellina* is famous for *Pizzoccheri*," Michele explained, completely missing the innuendo.

"What's *Pizzoccheri*?" I hadn't heard the word before.

"It's a type of pasta made from *Saraceno* flour and comes in long, thin strands that are a greyish colour with specks. Look." He picked up the packet to show me before continuing. "It's cooked with potatoes and cabbage. You'll love it." He was practically drooling. He forgot to tell me that a generous helping of melted butter with fried onion or garlic is poured over it and a special type of cheese called *Bitto* is sliced and mixed with it. To finish it off, a liberal amount of parmesan cheese is sprinkled on the top. However, for once, Michele was wrong. As his sister handed me my plate, I didn't quite know how I was going to eat it. The *Pizzoccheri* lay in a sea of butter and onion slices and the slivers of soft cheese fused together with the *pasta* made it lumpy and not exactly appetising for a novice. You definitely needed to acquire a taste for it. My mum aptly nicknamed it *rubber bands* and that's what it will always be for us.

*

From the very beginning, I cooked English meals as well as Italian ones. It came in handy especially when we invited friends or family for a meal who had never been to England.

"Cos'é questo piatto?" they'd ask sitting down to a plate of Cottage Pie.

"Buono! Mi dai la ricetta?"

If someone said it was good and asked for the recipe then I considered it a success.

Blackberry and apple crumble with custard usually had varying reactions from:

"No, grazie, sono sazio. Aspetto il caffè."

To: *"Wow! Questo sì è diverso. Dove hai comprato la roba gialla?"*

Which roughly translated means: "No, thanks, I'm quite full. I'll wait for coffee."

Or: "Wow! This is something different. Where did you buy the yellow stuff?"

If my beef casserole didn't turn out exactly as it should have, I could always say that we ate it like that in Poole. Hoping that any Italians venturing across the Channel would choose to eat in an Italian restaurant instead of sampling any British dishes I'd offered.

As soon as Alex and Elisa could eat solids, I introduced them to Marmite soldiers which caused a sensation. While my children munched through their *fingers* of soft rolls liberally spread with butter and Marmite, anyone who happened to drop in, looked suspiciously at the offending food. Smelling the jar, they wrinkled their noses and shook their heads in mock horror.

"Che puzza! Che cos'è?" To Italian noses, Marmite could be nothing but offensive.

"It's called *Marmite* and it's very good for children," I stated in my best Italian, daring any further criticism.

Another speciality which provoked varied remarks was *jelly*. How could this weird, wobbly, colourful dessert be nutritious? Alex and Elisa loved both of these delights, though and I served them up regularly.

My mother-in-law, Carla, suggested I gave Alex and Elisa a couple of dishes she'd given her children.

"Michele e suoi fratelli sono cresciuti mangiando spesso pan cotto e cervello; fa bene ai bambini," she told me.

"Che cosa sono?" I was curious to know what appetising dishes they were. I couldn't have been more surprised to hear her explanation.

"E' brodo fatto di carne o il dado e pane raffermo sciolto dentro."

I had no doubt that stale bread in a meat broth or with the equivalent of an Oxo cube had some nutritious value but when I found out the meaning of *cervello,* I decided my children wouldn't be eating *cow brain* in the near future. Michele was very slightly built and not exactly tall and although it was unreasonable to assume his constitution had anything to do with his diet, I intended feeding my children the best of both countries. I gave Alex and Elisa cereals for breakfast and tried to keep to a staple diet but they also enjoyed English snacks such as scrambled egg on toast, jacket potatoes, and cheese on toast.

Occasionally, Michele arrived home with a bag containing tomorrow's dinner.

"*Mamma* thought we'd like to 'ave one of the chickens she…" he stopped mid-sentence, realising that if he wanted me to cook it, perhaps it was better not to remind me where the poor bird had been a few days ago.

On my part, I deliberately tried to forget that I was salting and spicing one of my farm friends, nurtured lovingly by Carla, and considered it just another piece of meat. At such times, I couldn't help remembering my old friend, Porky, who had been a piglet when I first arrived. He'd grown into a fine specimen of a boar and with a piece of rope tied loosely around his neck, I'd often taken him for walks – such was my need for a companion at times. I hadn't foreseen his ominous fate, somehow totally ignoring the daily hints from the in-laws that Porky's days were numbered.

I had never considered for one moment that the pig I'd watched grow from a squealing, pink bundle into a gentle, lumbering adult would end up as pork steaks or sausages on our table. Needless to say, I declined Alberto's kind offer to assist in the demise of my animal friend and a lesson in salami making and took myself off for a long walk.

"I don't think we'll be keeping hens or pigs when we move into our new house," I told Michele.

"No," he replied, understanding exactly what I meant. It was one thing to buy meat from the butcher but to actually go into the garden and choose your dinner – no, thank you. A clucking hen or gobbling turkey would be quite safe with us on Christmas Eve or any other day.

Although I admired the way Carla made use of the land and farm animals, even stuffing pillows and cushions with the chicken feathers, I wasn't ready to follow her example. My Englishness, combined with the fact that I was brought up in a large town, came through with a vengeance and I preferred to buy meat from the butcher's and ready-made cushions from shops.

*

'I need to buy a kilo or more of patience,' I thought to myself as I threw away yet another culinary disaster but after several dismal attempts at making *maionnese* for Russian salad, I gave up trying, opting to buy a jar of it instead – but not so with my *béchamel* sauce for lasagne. I persevered until my roux sauce was as smooth as any Master Chef's.

"It's not lasagne, is it?" Alex asked, unbelievingly.

"Yes, it is. And I know it's taken me about ten years to perfect it but I think you'll find it's like *nonna's*," I said, crossing my fingers.

Three forks hovered, waiting for the other to try it first then their faces creased into astonished smiles.

"Mum, it's really good!" Alex said between mouthfuls.

"It really is, Mummy!" Elisa agreed.

"Certainly, it's like *mamma's*," added Michele.

Praise indeed from my husband and children. Unfortunately, the same could not be said for the meat for *spezzatino* – a sort of casserole cooked on the gas stove and eaten with *polenta*.

"Um, the meat's a bit chewy," Alex told me apologetically.

"No, it's very chewy," Michele wasn't known for his diplomacy.

If I really put my mind to it, my attempts at cooking improved incredibly and I surprised Michele and the children when they actually recognised a typical *Valtellinese* dish on the table that they could also eat and enjoy. However, mealtimes usually involved an element of the unexpected – depending on whether the menu turned out to be edible or I had to revert to Plan B – the family never knew exactly what I intended preparing. Both Alex and Elisa grew up with the mantra: *Don't be like me, learn to cook!* And they did. My sister is an excellent chef, so whenever we went to England or she came to visit us, the children watched her create appetising recipes in no time at all.

"Have you got any courgettes?" Diane asked the first time she came over in winter.

"No, you can only buy what's in season here," I told her, "and courgettes are ready to eat in the summer."

She wasn't sure whether I was being serious or not.

The arrival of supermarkets in our area in 1989 brought an air of innovation for several reasons: I had a better choice of fruit and vegetables all year; a wider range of products; items were cheaper; and shopping was quicker because the customer couldn't have a long chat with the cashier. Mind you, if I *happened* to bump into someone I knew in one of the aisles, and if the cashier *happened* to understand the conversation between

Elisa and me and confided that she'd been an au pair in Edgware for six months when she was eighteen, then I obviously stopped to chat and I could still take an hour or more to buy a couple of things on my list.

"With a bit of luck, it won't be long before chain stores open then I'll be able to buy clothes here without spending a fortune and feeling pressurised by assistants wanting to make sure I buy something," I told Diane as we walked out of the new Iperal supermarket.

I usually stocked up on clothes when we went to Poole in the summer because we arrived with the sales and always found great bargains. The sheer elation of being able to look freely at the garments without someone cajoling and complimenting on how well the garment fitted me regardless of whether the colour or style suited me, made me almost lightheaded. Not to mention the fact that shops didn't close for lunch and a siesta and you never saw a sign outside saying: *Back soon!* There was no denying it, I missed shopping in England.

13

Pass-the-Parcel

"Posso chiederle una cosa?" Alex's teacher called out to me as I chatted to Elisa during their break-time. I often saw them playing outside when I walked to the butcher's and usually had a few words with the teachers, too.

"Certo," I replied, wondering what she wanted.

"Lei sarebbe disposta a insegnare ai bambini inglese a scuola?"

I could hardly believe my ears. Alex's teacher was asking me if I'd be willing to give English lessons to the children at primary school at Mantello. She explained that if I was interested, the principal had suggested one afternoon a week when I could take two lessons, one after the other. Naturally, I jumped at the chance. Alex wasn't too keen on the idea when I told everyone over lunch.

"What do I have to call you if I want to answer a question: Mum or teacher?" He wanted to get things in perspective straightaway.

"Well, perhaps it would be better if you call me teacher or just nothing."

"What if I forget and call you Mummy?" Elisa asked.

"I expect everyone will laugh," I smiled at her serious face. "But it really doesn't matter. If you want to speak, just put your hand up like you usually do at school."

Despite their worries, the lessons went well, although several of Alex's friends remarked that I behaved like a teacher as soon as I walked into the classroom which made me smile. They were used to seeing me as Alex and Elisa's mum at home, not in teacher mode at school. I chose a text book with lots of games and songs as well as easy exercises, making the lessons as interesting and fun as possible and the children responded enthusiastically. It felt good to be back in the classroom and even though it only lasted a couple of hours, once a week for a few months, I hoped that one day, I'd find myself on the staff of a school once more. For the time being, I had to make do with sporadic English courses and the hope that one day, my teaching certificate would be acknowledged by the Italian educational authorities.

Alex, who was in the fourth year, didn't mind his mum standing at the front of the class after all. In fact, if anything, it made him even more Anglo-Italian.

"Mum, can I have a party like children in England?" he asked, a month before his birthday.

"I don't see why not," I replied, happy to think his English roots didn't lie forgotten.

"Can we have jelly and crisps and play games like *Musical Chairs* and *Pass-the-Parcel*?"

"If you want to," I said, wondering if Gaetana would be willing to give me a hand.

Elisa celebrated her birthday in England every year with a party in true English style, so it was only fair to let Alex have one, too.

I always had a few packets of jelly in the cupboard and I also found a trifle hidden away. Alex made invitations for his whole class and came home ecstatic when all the children accepted. His birthday was on a Thursday and as they had afternoon school, we decided to have the party afterwards and Gaetana said she'd be only too happy to help me.

I spent the morning of Alex's 10th birthday, making jellies and a trifle.

"Oh, Mum, it's going to be the first real English party in Piussogno," he smiled happily, sitting at the table. "I can't wait for my friends to come and see how we do it. Is dinner ready? I'm really hungry."

"Good. I'm glad you're not too excited to eat," I smiled back.

I drove them to school in the afternoon and then went to fetch Gaetana and Luana. We hung balloons around the house and then wrapped up prizes for Pass-the-parcel. At 4.30pm, the children arrived and after giving the Birthday Boy his presents, they sat round the table and sampled the English desserts I'd prepared. I have to admit to feeling slightly apprehensive as to whether his classmates would like the spread – I needn't have worried – they scoffed the lot.

The games proved a novelty, and although the actual task of sitting quietly and passing the parcel until the music stopped was a feat in itself for some children, they managed it.

"I should have done more parcels," I whispered to Gaetana.

"No, I think three are quite enough," she whispered back.

The noise level rose as they played Musical Statues – I decided that Musical Chairs might be too dangerous for the more boisterous guests – and then we played Stick-the-tail-on-the-Dog which was a huge success. Nearly two hours later, clutching their Party Bags, I took the children home. Nobody wanted to leave until I recklessly promised them a repeat performance the following year on Alex's next birthday.

"Thanks, Mum. It was great!" Alex's face mirrored his words. I couldn't have felt happier myself especially as an after-thought he said, "It's good being Anglo-Italian."

Alex's party was the talk of the village and those surrounding us. Parents stopped me to ask what I'd given them to eat and how to make it. They also wanted to know the games they'd played. Having moved out to the *suburb* of Piussogno, I was acutely aware of the villagers' keen interest in everything I did from how I dressed the children and brought them up, to how I'd furnished the house and my own behaviour and not for the first time, I felt proud to be English. I also realised that Alex and Elisa had English blood in them; they both developed a wicked sense of humour and Alex had a flair for telling jokes.

As they got older, they counted the days to our summer holidays in England and I quietly ignored the fact that perhaps I should also take them on holiday to the Adriatic coast with their paternal grandparents. Alex had his birthday in Italy with his Italian relations and Elisa celebrated hers in the UK with my family – it was quite fair. My sister always made a superb cake with a theme for her niece, whereas Alex had a plain sponge with castor sugar sprinkled over it – I did my best.

Obviously, Alex and Elisa had more contact with their Italian *zii* but I loved hearing them talk fondly about my family, too and see them get excited when they knew they were coming to see us or it was time to pack to go to England.

Alex was just four months old when he flew for the first time to meet my family. His big dark eyes and gummy smile won the heart of whoever looked his way and being held by people he'd only just met made him gurgle and laugh. Elisa had to wait until she was eleven months old before she took to the skies and her first flight wasn't as quiet as her brother's. Unfortunately for the passengers aboard, she exercised her lungs in a pitiful wail from take-off to landing. Nothing could distract her and after an hour and a half I began to have some very uncharitable thoughts regarding my daughter. However, I can happily say it proved to be an isolated case and future flights turned out to be normal, quiet ones.

As soon as school finished, Alex and Elisa said goodbye to family and friends and helped me pack their clothes and favourite toys to take to Nanna's.

The children looked forward to seeing their English relations; their aunts and uncles spoiled them totally and absolutely, taking them for day trips to theme parks or other places of interest at weekends.

"Mum, can we sleep at Andy and Debbie's tonight, please?" Alex asked.

"Please, Mum. We'll be ever so good, honestly!" Elisa added.

On other occasions, they'd ask to spend the weekend with my sister and her family in Fleet.

"Auntie Diane and Uncle Gordon said we can stay with them if we like."

"And we haven't seen Lindsey and Sean for ages." They always had an excellent reason for going and I knew they enjoyed playing with their younger cousins. Our English holidays became an annual event. I couldn't wait for this respite and often felt guilty for the lack of enthusiasm I felt when it was time to go back to Piussogno.

I found a job at the Anglo-Continental Language School in Bournemouth teaching English to foreign students which gave me the chance to keep up to date with the latest teaching methods and my mum looked after her grandchildren five mornings a week during July and August. Together with my aunt, they often organised a morning out for Alex and Elisa, while I enjoyed the challenges within the classroom and wished I could have found something similar in Italy.

When I finished my teaching stint, we'd drive down to Cornwall to spend a week at the Carbis Bay

Hotel, owned by my uncle. Alex and Elisa had great fun playing with their cousins in the sea and in the outdoor swimming pool, not to mention eating two fried breakfasts in the morning. They also made friends with children holidaying there and one summer they started speaking English with a Geordie accent after meeting two children from Newcastle.

Michele couldn't always follow us to England in the summer but my need to 'go home' to recharge my batteries over-rode my guilt at leaving him in Piussogno.

Besides, the Italian climate was far too hot for me during July and August and I didn't want Michele to see me wither in the heat. No, I much preferred the cooler alternative of an English summer.

14

Coffee, Please!

Chilly November days seemed to arrive unannounced and usually after a particularly frosty night when you wake up in the early hours of the morning, teeth chattering, cold and shivering, wishing you'd had the foresight to get out the winter duvet the day before. Despite my resolution to 'be prepared', I never was and it always took a touch of hypothermia to remind me to change the bedding. Busy with the job in hand, the sudden ringing of the phone made me jump.

"Pronto."

"Ciao, sono Emily. Vieni alla festa la settimana prossima?"

Emily wanted to know whether I'd be going to the annual Foreigners' get together the following week. This year, we were going to a restaurant at Traona, a village near Piussogno and I arranged to take Emily, my Spanish friend, a Venezuelan and a Mexican.

Imagine my surprise when the first car I saw in the car park was an English one.

"Guardate, una macchina inglese!" I felt quite excited. Perhaps I'd meet another English person. I got out of

the car in record time and walked quickly into the foyer with my passengers close behind me.

"Excuse me, but can you tell me who owns the English car in the car park?" I asked the barman without thinking.

"It's mine."

"What?" I couldn't believe it.

"My wife's English. We've just come over with our four daughters."

Well, that was it. I forgot about the meal and my friends – I wanted to know more about his wife. Gino gave me their phone number and the next day I rang Julie. We agreed to meet up in Morbegno.

"How will you recognise each other?" asked Alex after I'd regaled the family with the latest piece of news.

"We're English, we won't have any trouble finding each other."

And we didn't. We met outside the station and walked to the nearest *bar*, talking nonstop.

Julie lived with her family in Colorina, a mountain village even smaller than Piussogno, on the way to Sondrio. We couldn't believe it when we discovered that we'd lived quite near each other in the UK; I was from Poole, she was from Bournemouth – incredible!

"How come everyone in the village knows what's going on before it happens?"

"That's a good question." Being a veteran foreigner of thirteen years, it no longer bothered me. "Don't worry, you'll soon get used to it," I assured her.

"Really?" she didn't sound convinced.

"Two hot chocolates, please." The waitress looked at me blankly.

"You just ordered in English," Julie explained, suppressing a laugh while the girl stood waiting impassively, notepad and pen poised to take our order.

*

"I need to buy some Sellotape but I haven't a clue what it is in Italian and I forgot to ask Gino," Julie said as we walked out of the *bar*.

"It's *scotch*."

"What, like the drink?"

"Yes." I hadn't really thought about it before.

When we reached the shop, it was closed and there was a sign hanging up: *Torno Subito!*

"What does that mean?"

"It means *Back Soon!* and it also means we've got plenty of time for some window shopping before it opens."

"Are you saying that shops just close if they have to go to the bank or something? They hang a sign up and customers wait?"

"Yes, they wait – unless they're English, of course." She looked at me to see if I was joking or not.

"I've got a lot to learn, haven't I?"

My nod answered her question and we laughed.

We made a point of meeting up at least once a week for a coffee morning in Morbegno. Her husband, children and menagerie of one dog and five cats, together with my family and a cat, meant there was always something to talk about.

"Sorry I'm late," I apologised one morning. "But I ran out of road."

"What on earth are you talking about?"

"The road I always take to the station has been closed off and I hadn't a clue where the diversion was taking me."

She thought I was having just another bad hair day until it happened to her.

"You'll never guess, but I was driving back from Sondrio when the road ended. I had to follow the diversion route and what should have been a ten minute drive, took me forty minutes. Honestly."

"Coffee?"

"Definitely."

*

A few weeks later, my mother-in-law, Carla, popped in to see Elisa who was home from school with a nasty cold.

"Ha la febbre?" she asked.

"Non lo so," I realised I hadn't taken her temperature.

Carla touched Elisa's forehead before confirming that she definitely had a temperature.

"Prendi il termometro," she told me. I went into the bathroom to get the thermometer and then remembered I'd broken it and hadn't replaced it.

"Non c'è l'ho, devo comprarne uno," I confessed. I wanted to suggest getting a bag of frozen peas but decided to keep quiet. Elisa didn't get ill very often but when she caught

a cold or the flu, she invariably ended up being feverish for a few days. I still had to get used to the fact that every Italian household boasted a mini pharmacy. I usually managed to find an aspirin, disinfectant, and a packet of plasters. I had a feeling of déjà vu as Carla sent me off to the local chemist to buy a brand new thermometer.

On our next coffee morning, I asked Julie if she had remedies for every ailment in her house.

"You are joking, aren't you? If I need anything I go and buy it," she looked long and hard at me before adding, "I've always got a packet of aspirin, a tube of antiseptic cream and plasters."

"No thermometer?" I ventured.

"No, of course not. You can tell if someone has got a temperature or not."

Any sense of guilt I may have had, faded away at her words – I smiled and finished my coffee.

*

During school holidays, Julie and her family often came over for the day and while we drank tea in the kitchen, the girls played with Alex and Elisa, running around in the garden or disappearing upstairs to explore the attic.

"How long do you cook a *Bolognese* sauce for," I asked Julie.

"Why do you want to know that?"

"Well, most people I've spoken to say they cook it for at least two hours sometimes more. My sauce is ready in half an hour."

"You really don't like cooking, do you?"

"How did you guess?" I grinned. "Actually, I made the cardinal sin of telling some people that I often do other things like washing my hair or putting the washing on the line while I'm cooking. They couldn't believe I didn't stay in the kitchen watching everything bubble away until it's ready to eat."

"So, what's on the menu today then?" she asked.

"*Pasta?*"

15

Do, Re, Me

"Hai tempo per un caffè?" Silly question – I always had time for a coffee.

"Sì, certo."

Sure enough, ten minutes later my friend, Patrizia rang the bell and the conversation went like this:

"Ciao. I've been thinking about it a lot and I want to know what you think."

"Sì?" I had no idea what she was talking about.

"Grazie," she said, gulping her *espresso* before I'd even sat down.

"A choir. I want to start a church choir here, in Piussogno. What do you think?"

"Well, it's a good idea but how are you going to choose choir members?"

I couldn't help thinking of some of the congregation singing flatly to hymns during the Sunday service.

"That's not a problem. We'll have a meeting to discuss it and then choose an evening for choir practice." Her enthusiasm was almost tangible and we spent the next hour discussing the new project.

Patrizia decided to ask permission to hold the meeting in the primary school, in the square. Nearly all of the villagers turned out to see what *this choir business was all about*. After much debate regarding the evening for practices – it couldn't be held on a Wednesday because there were usually football matches on television, then the time – not before 8.30pm because a lot of people worked until 7pm and we had to take into consideration the fact that they needed to relax a bit after the meal – so, we settled for Tuesdays at 8.30pm in the church. On 15th February, 1991, Michele, Alex, Elisa and I went along, even though I suggested Michele stayed home. He has a great voice singing in the shower but elsewhere, it doesn't seem to have the same effect.

"Now, I want to hear all of you sing a few notes in order to sort out the voices," Patrizia said in Italian and not dialect. A few people started muttering and looking uncomfortable, others looked behind them to see how far away the door was.

She played the organ and asked a group of young women to sing. After much coughing and giggling, but no actual singing, she chose a different tactic. Catching my eye, she asked how many people played musical instruments and could read music. I put my hand up, so did Alex and Elisa and several young teenagers followed suit. I smiled encouragingly at Patrizia – it was a start. She forced a smile back then began playing a well-known hymn and everyone joined in. An hour and a half later, as we got ready to go home, Patrizia asked me to stay behind.

"Have I done the right thing?"

"Of course you have. It'll just take a bit longer to teach new hymns, that's all. Don't worry." I felt quite optimistic, that is until I found myself between two sopranos, who should have been contraltos and who sang their own thing regardless. I honestly didn't know whether to laugh or cry. Michele was a regular member until I winced once too often. At that point, he decided that maybe he should stick to his personal renditions in the shower.

With dedication and determination, Patrizia formed a choir of thirty men, women and teenagers and if not defined as a first class choir, no-one could fault the enthusiasm in the way the hymns were sung. Invariably, a soloist at some point gave a unique interpretation of the music.

"Listen, let's try and finish on the same note, shall we?" Patrizia suggested diplomatically.

Naturally, I became an ardent soprano and Patrizia's love of the English language meant that certain pieces in my mother tongue challenged the congregation and choir members alike. It's to her credit that she managed to transform a handful of people with little or no knowledge of music into a group that could tackle any piece of music with three or more voices. The choir became an important part of village life and we practised religiously for special festivals and even weddings. An air of expectancy filled the church as Patrizia took her place at the organ. What would the choir sing today? Our organist loved to vary her themes and we, her choristers, had to live up to her expectations. We'd be rewarded with a smile and a nod when we managed to give a relatively good performance, but if we missed our cue because we weren't paying attention or didn't sing with feeling, her look spoke volumes.

Her introduction of the Savannah adaptations for set pieces during the service brought an ethnic touch to it and as she swayed to the rhythm as she played the organ, certain choir members (no names mentioned) also found it incredibly difficult to keep still. Whoopy Goldberg's adaptation of Sister Act would not be amiss.

16

Flying High!

"Avete comprato un cavallo?" Too busy thinking about what I had to buy in the shop, I hadn't seen the woman in front of me.

"Oh, ciao. Cosa?"

"Avete comprato un cavallo?" she repeated her question. Why on earth did she think we'd bought a horse?

"Perchè?" I was curious to know why.

"Beh, cos'è quell'affare nel parcheggio?"

I had to laugh when I realised she was referring to our friends' camper with the microlight trailer behind it which stood proudly in the car park at the bottom of our drive. When Kathy went back to England, we promised we'd keep in touch and we did. She and Colin had trundled into Piussogno the day before to see us and word had already got round that there had to be a horse inside it. I decided to put the record straight.

"No, no. Non è un cavallo, è un deltaplano," I explained, but Rosa still wasn't any the wiser.

"Un...che cosa?" She didn't have a clue what I was talking about, so I resorted to gestures to help explain the

101

rudimentary microlights, which in fact looked more like flying chairs that we saw occasionally buzzing above us on clear days at weekends.

"Ah, quelle cose." A smile spread across her face as she finally understood what lay hidden in the trailer. We exchanged a few more pleasantries then I said goodbye and walked into the shop.

On this particular Saturday in December, 1991 as I did the shopping, Kathy and Colin drove down to Nuova Olonio, a local village where microlights could take to the air and began preparing for their flight. With the children home for the Christmas holidays, we arranged to meet them later.

"Mum, be as quick as you can. Don't stop for a chat…" as if I would.

By the time we joined our friends, the microlight was ready for take-off and several microlight owners stood around, giving it an appreciative eye. Compared to the Italian models, some which resembled tricycles with wings and others high-backed chairs, Colin's jet-like craft seemed much more superior, and he looked pretty impressive himself dressed in a bright red flying suit with goggles.

"Don't you think he looks like the infamous Red Baron?" Kathy asked us, laughing.

A watery sun in a bright blue sky did little to alleviate the chill in the air but with adrenalin racing through our veins, none of us felt the cold. Alex and Elisa couldn't wait to climb into the back seat and have a go – and neither could I. Michele, on the other hand, stood to one side, looking disconcertedly at the machine.

"*Vuoi provare anche tu, Papà?*" Elisa wanted to know if he was tempted to try.

"*Beh, non lo so. Magari non c'è tempo per far provare tutti.*" Maybe there wouldn't be time for all of us to have a ride but I had the feeling that Michele would forfeit his turn anyway.

"Who wants to go first, then?" Colin asked, ready for action.

"Can I, please? Then Elisa can go," Alex said as he tightened his scarf round his neck, pulled his beret over his ears, then adjusted his crash helmet before climbing into the back seat, his smile growing bigger by the minute.

Colin checked the control panel, switched on the engine, and as the motor revved quicker and louder, the microlight rolled forward, picking up speed before launching itself into the air. Gloved hands shaded eyes from the light to get a better view as we watched the craft disappear into the distance above the mountains. Twenty minutes later, Alex landed back in the field and reluctantly gave up his place to Elisa.

"It's fantastic," he enthused. "I saw our house and the river Adda and we went as far as Morbegno."

"Ready, Ellie?" Colin asked his next passenger.

"Yes, yes!" she replied happily, waving to us as Colin manoeuvred the microlight into position for take-off once more. Just as the aircraft gathered height, Alex chose that moment to enlighten his father on a few facts he'd gleaned from Colin during his ride.

"*Papà*, I asked Colin what would happen if we had engine problems or we hit something and if we'd have time to put life jackets on. He said we'd be quite safe in the air and would continue to glide – just the landing bit could be tricky."

Michele's face was a picture as he scanned the sky for his daughter in a bid to quash any irrational thoughts. Kathy and I couldn't help laughing.

"It's okay. Elisa will be fine," I assured him – and she was. Her face mirrored the euphoria she felt as she clambered out.

"It really is fantastic! Everything looks so small: houses, cars, the river. It's the best thing I've ever done," she said, enthusiastically.

"I've got enough fuel left for one more flight. Who wants to come?"

"Me! I'd love to have a go." I'm worse than the children, I thought to myself.

"Right, hop in, then," Colin told me.

I had conveniently forgotten that the higher you go, the colder it gets and I didn't have a scarf or gloves. As the microlight had no protection against the elements, a raw chill suddenly hit me in the face, spreading slowly through my body until I didn't know whether the trembling was due to the sheer excitement of it all or the low temperature. As we glided over the mountains, the beauty and tranquillity of the scene below us made any momentary discomfort worth it. I felt as if I was genuinely flying and at one with nature. Spotting a few landmarks, I pointed them out to Colin.

By the time we joined the others, my ears and hands were numb and my teeth chattered uncontrollably but it had been an experience of a life time.

"That was great. You don't know what you missed," I said to Michele.

"Oh, I think I do. You look very cold." He shivered, involuntarily.

"I'll take you next time, Michele," Colin promised.

Michele grinned and nodded. Somehow, I didn't think he would, though.

We invited them to stay for Christmas and they insisted on buying the turkey and cooking it. The idea of not having to put my culinary talents into practise more than appealed to me. What I hadn't bargained for was trying to fit an eight kilo turkey with all the trimmings into the oven.

"Wow," said Alex "that's some turkey." His eyes shone at the thought of it and his smile grew bigger by the minute. However, a week later, we still had turkey on the menu. We'd eaten it hot with boiled potatoes and vegetables, cold with salad, minced in a pie with chips and lastly, in a soup.

"Is that the last of the turkey?" Alex asked tentatively, his eyes shining a little less brightly.

"Yes, that's the last of it," Colin answered, almost apologetically.

"Ah," Alex breathed a sigh of relief and smiled.

All too soon, we had to say goodbye to Kathy and Colin. Their parting gift to us was an electric Polenta Maker. Most of the elderly locals still made *polenta* in what resembled a cauldron over a fire and even though it was becoming more popular to cook it on the gas stove, you still had to stir it continually with a wooden spoon. This present meant that I could do it myself without having to rely on Michele.

"Thank you!" I said, hugging them both.

"Every time you eat *polenta*, you can think of us," Kathy and Colin said before climbing into their camper.

I knew that both Alex and Elisa would miss them: they'd taught Alex to play chess and Elisa to ice skate but the children were used to saying goodbye to their English relations and managed to smile as Monty, the camper left for Southend-on-Sea. A few days later, the Christmas holidays came to an end, the children returned to their desks at school and life fell into its usual pattern.

17

Pot the Black Ball

Alex and Elisa finished their three years at middle school and then, after considerable consideration, chose to attend *Geometra* – the land surveyor senior school at Morbegno. Having been voted parent rep for both of them – principally because I'd been the only parent there on the day of voting (both times) – I had first-hand knowledge of what the teachers expected from their classes. Being used to the happy-family atmosphere of primary school, then the slightly more formal middle school, I found the distant rapport with most of the teachers at senior school quite daunting.

"Shall we have *merenda*, Mum?" Elisa asked.

"What? It's only 2.30pm."

"Oh, okay. I'll finish doing my homework then."

I looked at Elisa and wished she'd give me one of her sunny smiles. She was in her first year and Alex was in his third.

"Oh, come on. Who cares what time it is? Let's have a break now," I said.

Later, as we dunked our biscuits unceremoniously in our tea, I broached the subject of school again.

"You know, I loved going to Parkstone Grammar," I told Alex and Elisa who rolled their eyes at each other as if I were mad.

"We had a lovely rapport with the teachers, too," I added.

"What? Do you really mean that?" Alex asked incredulously.

"Yes, and we all cried on our last day."

"You didn't really, did you?" Elisa challenged.

"Look, not all schools are the same. I really enjoyed mine."

"I don't think I'll be crying on my last day," Elisa said.

"Not unless they're tears of happiness," Alex laughed.

I felt sad to think they didn't enjoy school as much as I had. They had both made new friends but neither of them looked forward impatiently to lessons or wanted to discuss various aspects of new subjects at mealtimes. 'Five years is a long time to dislike school,' I thought, and wondered for the umpteenth time if they had both chosen the wrong school.

I had to admit that I didn't relish the meetings at *Geometra*. I missed the cheerful banter between the teachers before they got down to the serious business of scholastic progress and performance in the classroom. Another obstacle was the language. I prided myself on being able to converse on any level in Italian but, until now, that hadn't included teachers at senior school. They apparently used a diction alien to struggling foreigners.

"I wish the teachers would use vocabulary that I understood instead of words I've never heard of before," I moaned to Michele after a particularly difficult meeting at Morbegno. "Perhaps I'll take a dictionary with me next time."

"Ma dai," Michele couldn't believe it had been that bad.

"Honestly, I missed half of what one teacher said because I was too busy trying to remember three new phrases."

"And what were they," Michele asked.

"I don't know, I can't remember," I couldn't help laughing.

I convinced myself that the next meeting would be fine and it probably would have been if I hadn't been so fascinated by the way one of the staff spoke without moving his lips.

"If he hadn't been like a ventriloquist, I'd have understood everything this time," I assured Michele.

"Sì, sì," he nodded, "certainly, you'll 'ave no problem next time."

Not sure whether he was teasing or not, I decided to let the matter drop.

*

The majority of new houses had a basement with a table and chairs and a fireplace where family and friends could meet up for a meal or eat roasted chestnuts without worrying about making the actual house dirty. The arrival of the pool table in our basement caused quite a sensation. Word inevitably got around that we had a professional one and naturally everyone was curious to see it. Michele's friends were suitably impressed and accepted invitations for a game.

"It's brilliant," I told Julie one morning over coffee. "We couldn't have chosen a better time to put the pool table together."

"Alex is sixteen, isn't he?" she asked.

"Yes, the age most boys are going to *bars*, but instead, he and his friends go down to the basement for a game."

Sometimes, a small group turned up to study but funnily enough, I usually heard the chink of the cues hitting the balls after a while.

"Well, who won?" I'd query when it was time to go home.

"How did you know?" They seemed genuinely surprised.

"I heard the balls upstairs," I answered.

"Ah," they'd say before looking sheepishly at each other.

I had to smile, if not the most academically orientated students, at least they were very happy, friendly boys.

Michele and I enjoyed a game of billiards with friends especially on a Sunday afternoon during the cold winter months when it could take hours trying desperately to pot the black ball.

"Time for *merenda*," I'd say and we'd stop for a cup of tea and a slice of cake before continuing the game. Invariably, our guests would still be with us when I suggested cooking spaghetti for everyone. I enjoyed these impromptu meals – even though it meant working a miracle in making a few rolls and some slices of cold meats into enough food for all.

Around this period, a miracle really did happen – Michele finally gave up smoking. The children and I sent up a silent prayer. His cough disappeared and he found a new lease of life which included the return of his taste buds. This proved a positive factor for him but meant he became food critic number one where my culinary efforts were concerned.

"Why didn't you sweeten the apple crumble?" he asked.

"I did but you've been *nicotine dependent* for most of your life and you're only just beginning to taste real food," I explained with all the patience I could muster.

"Did you forget to salt the pasta again?" he questioned on another occasion.

"No, I put in an extra helping for you," I countered, through gritted teeth.

At that moment, Carla popped in to see us.

"Che cos'avete mangiato?" she wanted to know what delicacy I'd served up for lunch. I felt very tempted to say: *insipid pasta – again!*

18

Translate, Please!

Many Italians emigrated to America and Australia in the early 1900s but despite the distance, kept in touch with their relatives *back home.* However, as time passed, not all the younger offspring learnt Italian and so I often had to translate letters, written in English, at Christmas and birthdays for the locals. Likewise, whenever anyone came from abroad to meet their extended family, they somehow ended up on my doorstep to enjoy a cup of tea and a chat – in their mother tongue.

I had just finished some much needed housework when the front door bell made me jump. I recognised the woman standing next to a young girl as the butcher's wife at Traona. She explained that her niece, Christine had come over from Australia for her cousin's wedding but she didn't speak Italian and needed someone to teach her – and they had thought of me. I thanked her for her confidence where my teaching ability was concerned but suggested she looked for a proper Italian teacher and Gaetana came to mind. She often corrected me when I used the wrong form of a verb. I could always offer cups of English tea and chats in Oxford English to Christine and I did. She stayed in Traona for a year enabling her to get to know her father's family and his roots, not to mention learning the language. She also came with me to the English course I was taking near Sondrio.

"This evening you're lucky enough to hear English spoken with an Australian accent," I told the group, as I introduced Christine. The students took to her immediately, and asked her to join in the lessons on a regular basis. At nineteen, she had a sunny disposition and a ready smile. Her enthusiasm to learn as much as possible during her stay was almost palpable and when it was time for her to return home, we knew we'd all miss her. We made her promise to come and visit us whenever she popped over to Traona – and – she kept that promise.

Over the years, the locals got to know other foreigners, namely my mum, brother, sister-in-law, my sister and her family and my aunt who were regular visitors as they walked around the village and greeted them as old friends. This time, my relations from Cornwall had come to visit and we were going to celebrate my 43rd birthday in Venice. Alex and Elisa had organised their weekend and were looking forward to some parental freedom.

As expected, our hotel on the Grand Canal, the food and excursion to Murano couldn't be faulted and the highlight was one evening in a restaurant which the concierge had suggested.

"I'm sure that's Marco Tardelli sitting behind me!" I nudged Michele, before explaining to my relations that he was a famous football player.

"I think you're right." Michele looked surreptitiously over my shoulder and nodded. "Yes, it's 'im."

When the waiter came to clear the table, I asked him for a piece of paper.

"Why did you do that?" Michele wanted to know.

"Because when he's finished drinking his coffee, I'm going to ask for his autograph."

"You can't do that," Michele whispered.

The waiter reappeared with a postcard of the restaurant, saying that was all he could find.

"Grazie mille, va benissimo," I thanked him, before turning to the table behind me.

"Scusi, ma posso chiederle un autografo, per favore?" I smiled, handing him the postcard and a pen.

"Certamente. A chi devo dedicare l'autografo?"

"Ad Alex, mio figlio." I knew Alex would be impressed with his autograph. He hadn't played for *Fiorentina* but he was still famous and had helped Italy win the World Cup in 1982. As he left his table with an extremely attractive woman, I asked if I could take his photo with Michele and he nodded, putting his arm around his shoulder and smiling for the camera. They had a quick chat about football and what he was doing at the time then he said: *"Arriverderci"* and left.

"What a nice man," my aunt said.

"He's quite good-looking, too," my cousin's girlfriend added.

Michele said nothing, relishing his chance meeting with a famous sportsman.

Imagine our surprise when we walked through the hotel foyer later that evening and came face to face with Marco Tardelli:

"Anche voi siete qui! Che coincidenza. Buona serata." He'd actually recognised us.

"Grazie. Buona serata anche a lei!" Michele managed to reply.

"Nothing like mixing with VIPs," I teased.

All too soon, we were back in Piussogno and it was time to say goodbye as my relatives left for Carbis Bay. We continued our usual routine: I had lessons to prepare for various courses organised privately by groups or by the council and school meetings to attend, in my role as parent rep for both children. I have to admit that I used to get very annoyed at parent-teacher meetings when I found myself constantly at the back of the non-existent queue. Impatient parents pushed and shoved in front of me in an attempt to speak to the teachers seated at tables around the room as quickly as possible. I had realised as soon as I stepped onto Italian soil that queuing was totally alien to Italians: getting off the plane, going through passport control, in shops, and of course, at school.

"Why don't you go instead of me?" I asked Michele after one particularly fraught afternoon spent at senior school.

"I can't. I 'ave to go to work," he smiled, indulgently. Men!

*

115

Summer came and went and I was enjoying a quiet chat with my mum, who happened to be over visiting, when I received an urgent phone call from Michele's cousin.

"*Ciao!* Can you come up to Cercino straight away? Some Americans are here and no-one can understand what they're saying."

"Don't worry, Remo, I'm on my way…"

Mum was only too happy to relax on the balcony and enjoy the scenery.

"I'll be back in time for a cup of tea – half an hour at the latest," I promised.

Unfortunately, it was a promise I couldn't keep and, if she hadn't made a pot herself, Mum would have had to wait nearly three hours for her drink.

It transpired that the Americans were, in fact, related to the cousins at Siro. The woman's grandfather was one of the uncles who had sailed to California at the beginning of the century. They were holidaying in Europe and had come to Italy especially to see if they could find his birthplace.

"Can you believe it, when I said I was looking for the Molatore family, this man from a place, I think it was Novate, suggested we tried Cercino – and here we are!" The new found cousin couldn't get over her luck at stumbling across her grandfather's home. It was an emotional reunion for both families. Since then, every so often they come over to visit, and I take on the role of interpreter. Considering herself more than lucky with this link from the past, *zia* couldn't believe it when another American cousin turned up several years later, thanks to a chance meeting with a relative in Fresno, California. This time, she met the granddaughter of the aunt who'd followed her brothers to America. She arrived with four friends in tow and I had the complex task of interpreting for five American women simultaneously.

"Life sure is full of surprises!" they said, while *zia* smiled affectionately at her newfound cousin.

With the discovery of their extended family, I wondered whether it might be an incentive for them to consider learning English – again. Years ago, Michele's cousin Remo and his wife, Lella came with a group to learn English. Remo arrived wearing the one-time regulation black school overall with a white collar, small haversack containing a notebook, pencil case and a banana for *merenda*. Needless to say, the lessons were hilarious and Remo, a born comedian, made my role as a teacher incredibly difficult; I spent most of the time laughing uncontrollably. Although it probably wasn't one of the most serious courses I've taken, it was certainly one of the most enjoyable.

"*Impareremo l'inglese quando andiamo in pensione,*" they told the latest relations who had come from Long Island to meet them.

As they won't be retiring for a while, I gathered I would still be interpreting for them in the foreseeable future.

19

Mamma Rocks!

'I can't say nothing ever happens in Piussogno', I thought as I sat down for a rare bit of me-time with a cup of English tea. I suppose it isn't every day that you come home to find a cow in your front garden. I'd only gone to the next village to do a quick shop and when I got back, as I walked up the drive, I was aware of an extremely large, brown shape by the roses in the garden.

'It can't be a cow – but it certainly looks like one.' I shaded my eyes against the sun and peered closer. 'Yes, it's definitely a cow! Shoo, shoo! Go away!' The cow glanced at me lazily before continuing to munch through a particular juicy part of the lawn. Michele was at work and Alex and Elisa were at school, so I had to deal with it on my own. Flapping my arms and screeching at the animal had little or no effect on it and after ten minutes my patience was dwindling. No way did I want a mound of fresh manure on my grass, either. 'Why can't we have a proper garden with a fence round it and a gate like other people?' I thought crossly to myself. Like a lot of men, Michele always *intended* doing it, he just never *got round to* doing it. Well, now is the time, I decided.

Certain that the cow belonged to the farmer who had a stable near the disco I went to find him but he was nowhere to be found. I glanced at my watch, if the pasta wasn't on the table as the bells struck twelve at least I had a credible excuse for once. I tried another tactic: 'Please go home', I spoke softly, making gentle movements to encourage the heifer to make its way back down the slope. Nothing, the cow wouldn't budge, seemingly very much at home in my garden and all I could do was wait for its owner. Eventually I saw him drive up the road and ran down to get him. Laughingly, he called out, *"Dai, Carolina, a casa!"* and off she lumbered.

"Devi chiamarla per nome, così torna alla stalla," the farmer explained. Had I known that all I had to do was call her by name, I could have resolved the problem myself. I was tempted to ask him for the names of the other cows – just in case it happened again. As expected, Michele's lunch was late but he didn't mind after hearing my dilemma. He promised he would put up a fence and more importantly, a gate that weekend. I mentally crossed them off my list of *Things to do.*

As if that wasn't enough excitement, a few days later, I had a phone call from Elisa's friend's sister whose boyfriend was an aspiring musician and DJ. She explained that he needed a female voice for a hardcore dance track he'd written in English and as they knew I sang in the local choir, they thought I could do it. She added that the recording would take place in a studio in

119

Milan. Forgetting that I had already celebrated my 43rd birthday and completely ignoring the reference to hard-core, I felt quite excited at singing on a CD and went to Mirko's house the following afternoon to meet Ivan. Nora proudly introduced me to her boyfriend who surprised me by speaking fairly good English. He explained that unfortunately we couldn't record in Milan after all and we would have to do it in Nora's room instead. While he set up the recording equipment, I took the opportunity to chat to her mum and caught up with the latest gossip in Mantello.

When they called me to say everything was ready, only then did reality hit me. Listening to the music while reading the lyrics, I felt my mouth go dry and my body temperature soar. Never being one to swear, no way could I repeat what Ivan had written.

"I'm sorry, but I can't sing this, or this, or even this," I said, pointing to the offending words.

"Oh," he replied, realising that I wanted him to change almost everything.

"Well, try singing it like this," he suggested, making the necessary alterations.

"Right." I adjusted the headphones and began again, conscious that I was singing this genre of music with a BBC accent. I also felt guilty at making Ivan revise the text he'd written. Then I had another thought: what would Alex and Elisa think? At nineteen and seventeen, it should be them doing it, not their mother.

"Look, are you sure you can't find someone else who can do this for you?" I asked, acutely aware of the fact that maybe I should have been home baking a cake instead of making a hardcore dance track.

"No, you're doing fine," he replied. "We repeat the first bit again before going on."

They offered me a cup of tea and biscuits mid-afternoon and then we continued until Ivan was satisfied with the end result. Admittedly, the music and the adapted lyrics were good but I wasn't so sure about my interpretation of it. No way did I want to be responsible for the demise of Ivan's career. He promised me he'd give me a copy as soon as it was ready and I came home.

"Where've you been, Mum?" Alex walked into the kitchen as I hurriedly got the dinner ready.

"Oh, just making a hardcore CD," I answered, as Elisa joined us.

"You what?" Two pairs of eyes stared back at me. "You're joking, aren't you?" Alex and Elisa didn't know whether to believe me or not.

"No, I'm not actually. Oh, don't worry, I'm not going to make a video to go with it." I couldn't help laughing as they looked at each other absolutely astounded.

"Mum, you do realise what hardcore is, don't you?" Elisa needed to know.

"Yes, of course I do. That's why I asked Ivan to change the words."

"Oh, Mum!" Alex's face was a picture of shock-horror.

"It's okay, you know I'd never do anything to deliberately embarrass either of you," I assured them as I fried four *cottolette* and washed the salad.

"I mean, would you be happier if I were a typical mother and stayed at home cleaning, washing and cooking?"

Again they exchanged looks before laying the table and I had a feeling that maybe it was better if I didn't know what they were thinking. Naturally, they couldn't wait for their father to come home.

"Papà, indovina che cos'ha fatto la mamma questo pomeriggio,"

"Scommetto che non indovinerai mai," Elisa added.

Michele looked at me then at his children.

"Allora? What 'ave you done this afternoon?"

"Oh, it's nothing much. I just sang for Ivan. Now, eat up before it gets cold," I said, attacking my turkey slice fried in egg and breadcrumbs.

"Mum, tell the truth," Elisa believed in plain speaking.

"It's true. I sang a track for Ivan."

"Papà, è hardcore. Hai capito?"

Fortunately, Michele hadn't a clue what they were talking about. Since the Rendez Vous had been rented out, Michele's disco days were over and he relied on the radio to keep up to date with the latest hits. I came to his rescue.

"I think what they're trying to say is that it's a type of music which isn't associated with someone of my age – and especially someone who is married with children. Am I right?"

"Mum, we know you're a working mum and usually we don't mind but singing hardcore like you teach

English, well, that's a bit embarrassing, isn't it?" Alex looked apologetically at me.

"And who said I sang it with a BBC accent?" I challenged.

"You always speak with a BBC accent," they almost spoke in unison.

"Just wait and see." I dared any further comments.

*

As soon as it was on the market, Ivan brought me a CD of the compilation with the Hardcore Generation track on it. He had mixed it so well and reworked my vocals that it sounded really good and I couldn't wait to play it to my family. Their reaction to it made me smile – they both gave me a hug and congratulated me.

"Well, Mum," Alex said proudly, "how many kids can say their mother made a hardcore CD?" Praise indeed!

Ivan's career took off and his music is played everywhere. Mind you, my vocation as a singer started and stopped right there...

20

A Day to Remember

"I can't believe that a pair of ordinary glasses costs so much," I moaned to Michele. Since my decision not to renew my contract at the language school in Bournemouth I had no more lengthy summer holidays with my family. Alex and Elisa now preferred holidays with their friends – and Michele couldn't take so much time off, either. However, it also meant that I could no longer rely on English opticians and had to find an alternative one in Morbegno. Although I'd got used to using the *lira,* the number of noughts on price tags still frightened me sometimes and today happened to be one of those moments. Up to now, I'd worn fashionable but not exceptionally expensive glasses from Specsavers in Poole High Street so being confronted with an abnormally excessive amount for a normal pair of Italian glasses made me livid.

"Morbegno has definitely lost points," I fumed. "I have never spent so much on my eyes before. Honestly, *seicentocinquantamila lire* for a very average pair of specs. I could go to Gatwick twice for that amount, if not more."

Michele chose to say nothing. I'd only recently decided that I'd have to look for another dentist as well. My English dentist, Mr Nicholls knew about my phobia for people in his profession and managed to talk me through fillings, impressions, and crowns but shorter visits to England now made dental appointments with him impossible. Several sleepless nights followed this decision and Michele wasn't sure how he could help me because he didn't go to the same dentist on a regular basis and he knew I didn't want to go back to *Dr Charming*, as I'd nicknamed the Italian dentist I'd gone to during my two pregnancies. I had to find one who had the same qualities as my loyal dentist in Parkstone.

"Well, at least I shouldn't have any more surprises on the health front," I said, but I was wrong.

A few days later, I had an appointment with the gynaecologist but instead of seeing the usual woman doctor, the nurse told me that Dr Calli would examine me. The name rang familiarly in my ears but it wasn't until I walked into the room and actually saw the doctor that I realised why. He was one of my students on the course at Morbegno.

"Ah," I managed to splutter.

"Ciao!" Recognising me immediately, the doctor smiled broadly, not at all embarrassed, and told me to get ready behind the screen.

"Um, I don't think so," I stammered, "I'll see you the day after tomorrow at the English lesson."

"Non è un problema per me, è il mio lavoro," he explained.

"Yes, I know it's not a problem for you, but it is for me." I tried to make light of the situation but I could only manage a forced smile.

"I'm not questioning your ability as a doctor, but as your English teacher, I'd prefer to wait and see Dr Spini as always. Bye." Not waiting for his reply, I opened the door as nonchalantly as I could and left.

Seeing my still flustered face when he came home, Michele asked what had happened at my appointment.

"Oh, nothing much. I walked in and out."

"Cosa? Perchè?" He couldn't understand what I meant.

"I mean, I walked in and the doctor was one of my students, so I walked out again."

"Ah," his smile spoke volumes.

I badly needed a diversion and Alex gave me one when he walked in later.

"Papà! La Fiorentina viene in Valtellina *in ritiro* – how do you say *in ritiro* in English, Mum? I've completely forgotten."

"I think it's: on retreat." I made a mental note to look it up, just to be on the safe side.

"My friends were talking about it. They're coming to Lecco to play a game then they're going to Bormio – on retreat." I couldn't remember seeing my son so excited. To say he was an ardent *Fiorentina* fan was an understatement but it was good to see him smiling again after the stress of end-of-school exams.

"Per'aps we can go to see them play," Michele suggested after reading that the team planned to go to

Sondrio, too. Needless to say, football happened to be the only topic of conversation for the following weeks and I couldn't wait for them to go with Michele's nephew, his cousin and his boys to see their idols on the pitch.

Nothing could have prepared me for the surprise when they came home – instead of being satisfied with their *Viola* afternoon, they started discussing the possibility of a family day out to the place mentioned for the team's retreat.

"We could go to Bormio tomorrow to see the players practising and then watch the friendly game against Grosio," Alex suggested.

"But what if they're going back to Lecco tonight," my thirteen year old nephew added. "We don't know for sure where they're staying."

"If it's in the papers then it should be true," Alex reasoned.

After listening to them anguish over the dilemma of not knowing whether the team was going back to Lecco or Bormio, I suggested ringing the Palace Hotel in Bormio where the *Fiorentina* team was supposed to be staying. In my best Italian, I pretended to be a sports reporter wanting to know if the *Fiorentina* team would be staying at the hotel for a few days and the receptionist replied in the affirmative. I earned a spontaneous kiss from Ricky, my nephew.

We set off early the next morning in two cars with Pietro and his family and Mara's oldest daughter. We found the stadium and watched the training session for an hour. I have to admit feeling excited seeing the players and the trainer in the flesh. As it was a warm summer's day, we decided to have a picnic in the mountain above Bormio by the Cancano Lakes before going back to the Palace Hotel in the afternoon.

When we arrived, there were a number of reporters gathered outside and I decided to join them. Telling my nephew to stay close to me, I marched up to the front of the hotel and when the concierge came out I spoke in English, saying I'd come from England to interview Giovanni Trappatoni. Fortunately, he didn't speak English and had no idea what I was saying.

"*Un momento, prego,*" he gestured for me to wait and darted inside the foyer to reappear a few minutes later with none other than the trainer himself.

"Hello. I've been following *Fiorentina* for a number of years and I wanted to meet you and the players," I explained.

"Are you from London?" Trappatoni asked, in very good English.

"No, I'm from Poole, in Dorset on the south coast," I said, giving him the *Fiorentina* book to autograph.

"Oh, I don't know Poole," he smiled, handing me back the book. "Thank you for coming. Bye."

"Thank you very much," I replied. "Bye."

No way could I be rated as a good news reporter but Alex managed to photograph me talking to him and Ricky remained speechless. We walked back to the stadium and took our seats, ready to watch the match and I could hardly keep still. I realised that I, too had well and truly got the *football bug*.

At half–time, I took my nephew to the area where the players were resting and giving autographs to fans. We saw a number of boys climbing over a fence in order to get a closer look but we automatically made our way to the gate and waited. A lady standing nearby heard me explain to Ricky that it wasn't right to do what they were doing and came over to talk to us.

"Siete di Bormio?" she asked.

"No,non siamo di Bormio." I told her we weren't from Bormio but we had come a long way to see our favourite team. She thought for a moment then asked me if we'd be around later that evening. I automatically said yes, to which she introduced herself as one of the organisers and told me to take Ricky to the Palace Hotel at 9pm and she'd let him in to meet the players. Without thinking, I asked her if my son could come, too. For once, my ability to talk to anyone and everyone had paid off. The second half passed in a blur and when both teams filed out to go back to their hotel, we decided to have something to eat. We found ourselves in an empty pizzeria in the town centre but when the owner finally came out of the kitchen and we told him there were nine of us, instead of being happy to have some customers, he said we were too many and couldn't cook for all of us. Absolutely dumbfounded, we left, opting for a toasted sandwich and a hot chocolate in a crowded *bar* nearby.

True to her word, at precisely 9pm, the woman came to the hotel entrance and took Alex and Ricky inside. I wished I'd asked if my husband could have been part of the group, too as Michele eagerly watched them talking to *Cois, Chiesa, Batistuta* and *Toldo*, to name but a few of the team, through the long windows. After a while, the woman came to the door again and beckoned to me to send Elisa and my nieces in, as well. Alex took photos of them together with the players, got their autographs and even joined in singing with Batistuta. It was an experience of a lifetime for them and 19th July, 1999 will always be a day to remember.

"Mind you," Alex told us confidentially afterwards on the way home, "Gabriel Batistuta can't sing for a toffee!"

21

A New Look

"Ellie, do you need the car this afternoon or can I have it?" Alex asked.

"If you're going to Morbegno, you can give me a lift," my daughter said before adding, "I want to see Luana."

I stopped what I was doing and looked at my children, remembering the day when Alex came home grinning and waving his driving licence.

"Well done, darling," I'd said, giving him a hug. "I knew you'd pass."

Two years later, history repeated itself with Elisa receiving a hug and a kiss as she joined the ranks of young motorists.

Whereas over the years I'd watched my children evolve miraculously from chubby toddlers to teenagers who now took it in turns to drive the family car, I couldn't say the same for our village. It had been a slow and silent metamorphosis but Piussogno was gaining a new look: people from Milan – *Milanesi* – bought and restructured old stables and buildings, turning them into fashionable holiday homes; modern terraced houses popped up like mushrooms and charming one-storey houses materialised. Noticeably, more cars appeared on the roads, which inevitably needed widening to carry the ever increasing traffic, and the sight of mules pulling carts laden with hay or logs became a memory. Pavements finally lined the roads, too late for me, but a welcome accessory for young mothers with pushchairs.

"Well, Piussogno looks very different from the last time I saw it," my sister commented as we sauntered down to the village square. "And where's the old washing trough?"

"They demolished it in order to make more room for parking," I explained, before stopping to chat to a young woman with a pushchair.

"I suppose you know everyone living here now," Diane said almost wistfully.

"Yes, I do." I took it for granted these days. Then I thought of something else.

"And have you noticed that you don't see dogs chained up outside anymore, left out in all weather?"

"Do you mean that cats and dogs have finally become part of the family?" she couldn't believe it.

"Yes, they're real pets, and are allowed indoors."

"Wow, at last!" she smiled.

Very subtly, the antiquated hamlet had become a modern day village or so it seemed. The overall structure gave the idea of progress but the mentality of some of its older male residents still resisted total change: they couldn't contemplate helping with domestic chores or preparing succulent meals. They worked on the vines, probably the last generation to do so, went to the *bar* for coffee and played cards, smoking their non-filter cigarettes until closing time. They vetted newcomers, watching them surreptitiously from a distance and new-fangled machines such as mobile phones and personal computers meant nothing but trouble. However, the younger generation flourished with the enthusiasm of enterprise: students enrolled at university instead of choosing manual work, women chose to follow a career, and the young people who had left their hometown in their teens, returned, ready to settle down with a family.

At this point, I suddenly realised that my son had stopped chatting to me whenever he had any spare time, spent longer in the bathroom before going out, smiled practically all the time, and asked if he could use the car more than usual. 'It's a girl,' I thought. 'It has to be a girl!' And, of course, a mother's instinct never fails – even if she's living on foreign soil. Alex introduced us to a pretty girl with deep blue eyes and long, light-brown hair, one Sunday afternoon.

"Mum, *Papà,* I'd like you to meet Lorena," he said, proudly.

They'd been classmates before becoming a couple, and seeing them laughing with their heads together, I knew he'd found his soul mate.

Little did we know that Alex's future wife had actually been in the baby unit, called *il nido* (the nest) with him at Morbegno Hospital. As is the custom, we met Lorena's parents, Dina and Angelo, and their two other daughters. Dina told us that she remembered the *Inglesina* who had given birth to a *bambino grande*, and was in the room next door to her. Lorena was born five days after Alex and had been in cot number 14. Dina, like me, enjoyed a good natter and we hit it off immediately, just as Michele and Angelo did. When we met up, the men went down to the basement for a game of pool while we stayed upstairs talking. I often popped in to see them on my way home from Morbegno and we exchanged local gossip over an *espresso*.

Alex left school as a qualified land-surveyor but instead of continuing his studies at university, he decided to help his father in the building trade while he waited to be summoned to do his military service. Conscription still existed in Italy and unless you asked to do social work, you had to spend ten months at a military base. The topic of the moment was naturally the Millennium and mass media talked of nothing but the *Millennium Bug*. Companies and small firms worried that something ominous could happen to computers with the coming of 2000 and many had already hired trouble shooters to fix any problems that might occur. My main worry was another: to go to England to see the New Year in or not to go. Diane and her family helped me with my dilemma by deciding that they would like to come to Piussogno to celebrate the new Millennium together with Mum and Auntie.

The following weeks flew by preparing English lessons, looking after the house and the family – not to mention coffee mornings with Julie and Gaetana – and before we knew it, we were at Malpensa airport waiting for our visitors to arrive.

I felt really happy to think I'd be celebrating with my English family for once. It meant that they would be able to see the *Live Nativity* at Cercino on Christmas Eve. A few years earlier, a small group of local people organised the reproduction of the biblical village of Bethlehem with huts where you could see people depicting various trades, in the square at Piussogno. It was so successful that they decided to put on a bigger pageant at Cercino the following year. Alex and Elisa were asked to be Mary and Joseph and I let them wear proper Arab clothes that a student from Abu Dhabi had given me. (My colleagues at the Anglo-Continental had teased me at the time that I'd arrive at school one morning to find a camel as a present.) Elisa rode on a donkey and whereas during rehearsals, they had been given a doll to hold, on the evening, they were presented with a real baby who fortunately for them slept the whole time. We found out later that Baby Jesus was actually Michele's cousin's two month old daughter.

"It's absolutely lovely," Auntie said, enthralled as we walked around looking at the carpenters sawing, the women spinning, others making butter. A lot of time and energy had gone into preparing the *Presepe Vivente* but it was worth it.

Next on the agenda after Christmas, was New Year's Eve and while Diane and I decided on the menu, the men discussed the entertainment.

"You want to come with us to buy fireworks?" Michele asked Sean and Gordon.

"Yes, okay." They both fancied a trip to Morbegno.

An hour later, they came back laughing and Gordon could hardly talk.

"What's the matter with you?" Diane wanted to know.

"You won't believe me if I tell you," he managed to say. "We chose some really good fireworks and when we went to pay for them, the cashier only had a lighted cigarette in his mouth..."

"What?" Diane didn't know whether to believe him or not.

"Shall we go to Iperal?" I felt we badly needed a divergence.

That evening, standing on the balcony, wrapped up against the crisp cold air, we saw fires glowing in the mountains and at midnight, fireworks lit up the night sky in a spectacular display. Thanks to Michele and his helpers, our own contribution made a fair impact on the welcoming of a New Millennium.

*

"Mum, I'm ready." Alex stood in front of me with his bag at his side and his hand in Lorena's who had offered to drive him to the station. More used to laughter and playful teasing in our family, I now had to fight back unfamiliar tears that risked spilling out at any moment.

"Off you go then," I said briskly, giving him a quick hug and peck on the cheek, "and don't forget to ring me when you get to Belluno."

"I won't," he grinned.

I watched them climb into Lorena's car and disappear down the road before turning back to the house. My son had left to do his military service at San Candido on the Austrian border.

"Cheery up." Michele invariably gave his own interpretation of well-known phrases but it made me smile.

"I'm not sad because he's going away – well, I'll miss him, obviously – it's just that to me, it's a waste of time and money, this conscription business."

"Certainly, for you it is, but for us it's good. It makes you stronger in character because you're by yourself, you 'ave to think for yourself and stand up for yourself."

I wasn't convinced; I'd have preferred Alex, a pacifist at heart, to do something more constructive for ten months instead of playing soldiers. Naturally, I only shared these thoughts with Gaetana and Julie. However, when Alex came home on leave in his *Alpini* uniform, he looked extremely good-looking and I felt more than proud to be his mother. He also looked remarkably well.

"I'm working in the office in San Candido – in the logistic department – helping to sort out the finances for the Sixth Regiment," he explained to us. "It's not so bad, Mum," he added.

He came home nearly every weekend and regaled us with stories of what *i nonni* (the soldiers in their last few months) made the novices do as penances. Sometimes, I didn't want to believe what I was hearing but Alex seemed happy enough – apart from the fact that he missed his girlfriend.

"I've got my *Giuramento* soon," he told us one Friday evening as soon as he arrived.

"What's that?" I hadn't a clue what it was.

"It's my *Swearing In* ceremony where all this year's recruits swear allegiance to the country. It's on Saturday, 11th March at the Rossi barracks in Merano."

I made a note of it on the calendar – not that I could forget such an important date.

"Piangerai sicuramente," a friend told me, *"è molto commovente."*

"I won't cry," I told her, "I'll be too proud of my son to cry.

"Vedremo, secondo me, piangerai – e tanto!" she nodded, absolutely convinced that I'd be overcome with emotion during the ceremony.

I hate to admit it but she was right. As the bugler played his poignant notes and the soldiers shouted their allegiance, there wasn't a dry eye to be seen. A shout from one of the officers was a signal for the soldiers to break ranks and run to their families.

"How are we going to find Alex in the crowd?" I wailed. I'd quite forgotten that he and Lorena had arranged a vantage point. Michele, Elisa and I stood together with Lorena, her parents, sister and uncle waiting for Alex to appear and we didn't have to wait long before he was smiling in front of us.

"Come on, let's take some photos, then." Elisa started snapping away.

A serious photo shoot followed of everyone together with Alex then Michele made a suggestion:

"Time for lunch, I think!" And it was.

22

I Do!

Life rolled by in a daily routine of looking after the family, teaching, choir practices, and meeting friends for coffee and a chat. Elisa left school as a qualified land-surveyor like her brother and Lorena before her, then decided to substitute the drawing board to giving massages and took a Shiatsu training course. I was only too happy for her to try out her techniques on me – I couldn't think of anything better than relaxing for an hour as she pummelled away the stress to the melodic strains of Native American music.

I had just finished one such idyllic session and felt very at peace with the world when Alex walked into the kitchen. He'd finished his military service and was back helping his father and uncle in their building business.

"Mum, *Papà* gave you an engagement ring, didn't he?"

"Yes, but I had to choose it myself first and then march him to the jewellers to buy it. He didn't think it was necessary but it meant a lot to me. Why do you ask?"

"Well, I'd like to buy one for Lorena and give it to her for Christmas," he said, almost shyly.

We knew that Alex and Lorena were officially a couple but I never thought that Alex would want to give her a proper ring as was the case in England.

"That's a really nice idea," I told him. "It'll also be a novelty for everyone here, too."

He chose a very delicate ring which I knew would look lovely on Lorena's slender finger. Now, I said to myself, Alex is the first Anglo-Italian in Piussogno to give an engagement ring to his girlfriend. As foreseen, Lorena loved her ring.

*

All through the evening meal, Alex kept looking up and grinning. I wondered if I'd got sauce on my cheek or I'd put my jumper on back to front, but no, everything was as it should be.

"Mum, what day is 29th September this year?"

"I don't know." I got up to get the calendar. "Oh, it's a Saturday. Why do you ask?"

"Well," he said carefully, "Lorena and I want to get married."

"Darling, that's fantastic news." I jumped up and hugged him. "And where are you going to live?"

"Actually, we wanted to ask you if we could have the flat upstairs?"

"Of course you can, no problem." I'd completely forgotten about my resolution years ago of not having a son of mine living above me in the same house.

They confirmed the date with the priest at Traona for their wedding and then joined a group at Chiavenna for the obligatory pre-matrimonial course. Lorena started looking at possible wedding dresses in numerous brochures but couldn't find anything she liked. In the end, she decided to have one made to her own requirements. As soon as planning permission was given, Michele and Alex set about transforming my upstairs store-room cum-laundry room where Alex and Elisa had often played with their friends in the past, into a fashionable family flat. Michele and I suggested they had a separate entrance but they designed the rest. While the men hammered and drilled, I worked in the garden, coaxing the plants to blossom and begging the weeds not to take over the rockeries. Alex asked me to go with him to buy his wedding suit and Lorena included me on trips to the florist and also for dress fittings together with her mother. Their flat materialised before our eyes and as the date drew closer we couldn't have been more excited, that is until the news of the terrorist attack on the Twin Towers hit our screens. In the face of such horror and destruction, we felt guilty to be so happy.

*

The weather forecaster had predicted rain on the day of the wedding and despite my theory of mind-over-matter, I couldn't stop the showers. Having said that, the happy couple only had eyes for each other and my family were suitably impressed with the priest officiating in sunglasses (a necessary accessory because he'd recently had his cataracts removed) not to mention his bushy grey beard and ample frame which gave him a familiar air. A visiting priest from Kenya who spoke English, kindly prolonged his stay so that he would be present at the wedding to translate during the service for Alex's relations from Poole and Cornwall – a gesture that was very much appreciated.

Alex's two witnesses arranged to drive him to the parish church at Traona in a vintage car owned by the father of one of them. As I had to accompany Alex up the aisle in my role of mother of the groom, I went along, too. At the bottom of the road, Davide stopped the car.

"Do you want me to go left or right? You've still got time to change your mind, you know," he joked.

Standing at the church door, waiting for the photographer to give us the signal to walk up the aisle, I remembered my own wedding, thinking that it had been a new chapter in my life and now, here I was, about to accompany my son on his. 'Goodness', I thought, 'I am getting sentimental after all these years living here'. My Italian friends said that I'd surely shed a tear or two but I didn't, although I have to admit to having a large lump in my throat when Alex and Lorena exchanged their vows. I also disappointed several people by not wearing an elaborate hat but fortunately, two of Alex's great aunts did and provided amusement for his friends who tried to see who could throw the most rice onto the brims. My Anglo-Scottish nephew, Sean, turned heads when he walked up the aisle in his kilt and Alex's friends couldn't wait to lift it up to find out whether or not he was a true Scot.

The reception held at a restaurant nearby, caused raised eyebrows when the non-Italians scrolled down the menu of no less than sixteen courses.

"We're not going to eat all this, are we?" they asked.

"Oh, yes!"

They had already commented on the buffet we had prepared for Alex's guests before going to the church.

"It'll take all afternoon to get through this menu," Andy said, and as always, he was right. In fact, we sat and ate all afternoon until early evening. In between courses, Alex and Lorena walked up and down the tables talking to guests, presenting them with the traditional *bomboniere,* a gift with five sugar almonds and a thank you note from the newlyweds and then we organised a couple of jokes to play on the Bride and Groom. As the rain stopped, we had a firework display outside which lit up the grey, dark skies in a kaleidoscope of colour and sound. Then everyone joined the happy couple as they took to the dance floor for the first dance.

As is the custom, Alex's friends and Elisa left quietly during the evening to prepare jokes in the new marital home. They blew up lots of balloons and filled the entire flat with them and afterwards, coming down the steps outside, they wrapped ribbon around the railings from one side to the other making it difficult to walk up or down.

"Is it time to go home, yet?" my sister asked hopefully, just before midnight.

"No, it isn't," I told her. "The party will continue in our basement."

"You are joking, aren't you?"

"No, no. In fact, the party will probably go on until the early hours of the morning."

"I want my bed," she said with feeling.

That year, on 29th September 2001, we celebrated Michele's Saint's Day together with Alex's wedding and we did it in style – the last of the guests left just after 5.00am.

My aunt had made a proper English wedding cake for the occasion which we decided to keep for the following day. Alex and Lorena cut it as we all sat round the table and this time it was the English members of the family who watched the reaction of the Italians, nibbling a small piece gingerly before nodding in agreement that it tasted delicious. They wanted to know what the ingredients were and how to make it then we toasted the newlyweds not with a cup of tea, but with sparkling wine – in true Italian fashion.

*

Before the English contingent flew home, we took them to ChocoAlpi, a chocolate shop nearby that Michele's cousin's husband had recently opened with the help of his family. They gave us a tour of the factory showing us how the chocolate was made and everyone appreciated the different samples offered.

"This is like 'Charlie and the Chocolate Factory'," Sean said.

We all left with bags of delicious flavoured chocolate and the promise to see them again – very soon!

23

Techno Mum

"I can't believe it's our Silver Wedding this year," I said to Michele. "Where has the time gone? We'll have to do something special."

"Yes. Like what?"

"Like – going to Rome. I still have to see the capital," I reminded him. "I know, we could celebrate before our anniversary and go with Dina and Angelo in August."

I knew that they'd jump at the chance and they did. Before Michele had time to change his mind, we'd booked a hotel near Termini station and seats on the *Freccia Rossa* train from Milan to Rome which supposedly took only four hours but on our journey, there was a two hour delay on route due to technical problems. However, nothing could spoil our special holiday. We spent the weekend of *Ferragosto* visiting the famous sights of Rome on our itinerary and despite the intense heat, walked everywhere and saw absolutely everything. It was fantastic.

"*Roma è stupenda.*" We all agreed with Dina. Wherever you looked, you saw and breathed history. As we threw a coin in the Trevi Fountain, we each vowed to return.

Back home again, I continued giving English lessons and preparing endless exercises on my well-worn battered typewriter.

"It's time you joined the twenty-first century and invested in a pc," my brother told me. I knew he was right but I was scared of change and afraid I wouldn't be able to use one. It had been difficult enough to adapt to the new currency at the beginning of the year when we stopped using *lire* and used euros instead.

I finally made up my mind after our anniversary celebrations in November while Andy and Debbie were with us, and asked them to accompany me to buy a computer. Back home, as Andy explained the rudiments to me, I felt the panic rising.

"I'm never going to learn." I honestly thought it was beyond my comprehension.

"Of course you will," Andy said. "It just takes time."

By the end of their stay, I had mastered the principal functions but I still didn't consider myself confident. I could always ask Alex in dire circumstances but I wanted to work it out myself and the main reason was that I didn't only need it for lessons. After a chance meeting with a well-known editor in London earlier that year, it had been suggested I tried writing a book about my initiation to a new life in a mountain village in northern Italy and the obstacles I had to overcome. As a complete novice, I wanted to do it on my own which would have been possible had I remembered my brother's advice to save everything. Instead, I would write for two to three hours and then press the wrong key and miraculously delete my work. At that point I'd hear Michele's voice:

"E' pronta la cena?"

"No, dinner isn't ready," I'd answer through clenched teeth.

In the end, Ivan came to the rescue. He rang me asking for conversation lessons and I asked him for computer lessons. He showed me how to save my work, how to make charts for lessons, and send and receive faxes.

"Call me if you need me," he said. And I did, on many occasions. I named him my PC Wizard.

Debbie sent me a manual which helped with the basics and gradually, I became more confident using the pc. Unfortunately, this meant I had less time to spend doing the gardening and while I improved my computer skills, the weeds ran wild and the grass grew longer.

Alex and Lorena came down grinning one evening to give us some very special news.

"Lorena's pregnant!" he told us. "You're going to be grandparents!"

Our granddaughter, Giulia arrived one snowy day in February, a beautiful baby with huge brown eyes and a mop of jet black hair. After that, the garden became a memory because I had no more free afternoons. When I wasn't writing, preparing or giving lessons, I was admiring my granddaughter growing from a contented baby into an inquisitive toddler.

"Mum, guess what, Giulia's going to have a baby brother or baby sister." Alex's smile said it all. Now it was my turn to smile.

"Did you know already?"

"No, of course not. It's just that the plant on the stairs flowered and grew another shoot when Giulia was on the way and the same thing has happened again."

'I'll have to call it the *Life Plant*,' I thought to myself.

Fabio made his debut in May and although he had a more difficult birth than his sister, he soon made up for it. I now had two grandchildren to keep me busy and I decided that it was time to invest in the Internet so that I could send emails and photos and Skype my family in England. Naturally, I asked Ivan who not only set it up but patiently talked me through it, as well. When I received a digital camera for my birthday, I was soon printing off photos, enlarging them, emailing them, you name it, I did it. Alex and Lorena gave me a Digital frame for Christmas, so I could put my photos on it and then slip it in my bag to show my friends.

Not long afterwards, Elisa introduced us to her boyfriend, Cristian who lived in the next village and we met his parents: Giuliana and Federico and his three brothers and their families. This naturally involved more Skyping, more photos and more emails to send to my family and for some reason, I earned the nickname *Techno Mum*.

24

All in the Name of Sant'Antonio!

"Prendi, porta tu la croce," Milena said, passing the heavy ornamental cross into my hands.

"Va bene," was all I could say. I could hardly believe what was happening as we filed out of church. For years, I'd watched the women who play a fundamental part in the church festival in June, lead the procession around the village to celebrate *Sant' Antonio*, the patron saint of Piussogno. Now, it appeared, I was to have that honour. It also signalled the fact that I had been fully accepted into the community. Raising the cross, I walked solemnly ahead of the statue, thinking back to the impact I'd made on the people when I first arrived.

Michele had not only brought a foreigner to Piussogno but an *Inglesina* who was also a confirmed Protestant – for the locals, not being Catholic meant I couldn't be a Christian. I assured them I was and if and when we had children, they would be baptised as Catholics. Peace reigned once more in the village and in time, Alex and Elisa attended catechism lessons and I even became a catechist.

"I've been asked to prepare a group of children for their First Communion," I told Michele when he came home for lunch.

"So? What's the problem?"

"Well, I'm Protestant, for one thing," I said, handing him a plate of pasta.

Don Giulio had finished his period of ten years in our parish and had been sent elsewhere. Don Paride had taken his place and had met Alex first when he acted as altar server for Sunday Mass.

"This is my mum – she's Protestant." Alex had introduced me to the new priest at the end of the service.

"Piacere," he smiled down at me before adding, *"Protestanti o Cattolici, abbiamo lo stesso Dio."* Yes, I thought, we do have the same God.

I took to him immediately which is why I found myself in this present dilemma – I hadn't had the courage to say no when he asked me to become a catechist.

"Certainly, everyone knows you're Protestant but if they are 'appy for you to teach their children and the priest is 'appy – do it."

Why was everything so easy for Michele? Several sleepless nights followed before Gaetana sorted me out, together with a dose of common sense from my mum. I mean, it wasn't that I didn't know anything about it. Both Alex and Elisa had already taken their First Communion.

I began my first lesson with six children, with butterflies in my tummy and a very dry mouth, but they proved to be an extremely well-behaved group of nine year olds and I soon relaxed. Once a week, we met for an hour in the church hall and discussed various aspects of Catholicism. Sometimes, Don Paride joined us for the last ten minutes. Before we knew it, the day came for the children to receive their First Communion and I felt privileged to have been an active part of it.

A few years later, Lory and I prepared a group for their Confirmation. This time, the group was larger and livelier and we were both delighted when the time came for the candidates to be Confirmed and we retired gracefully from the circle of catechists, preferring the easier job of cleaning the church.

*

While the children were growing up, I didn't have much time to dedicate to church affairs but we always went to *La Festa di Sant'Antonio*, our church festival in Piussogno, which takes place on the second Sunday in June. After the morning service we all watched expectantly as a man climbed onto a chair and began auctioning cakes and wine.

"Come on, now. Who will pay twenty thousand *lire* for this cake and a good bottle of red wine?" He shouted out a price and hoped someone else would start bidding. I gathered it was an important part of the festival.

We went to Vespers at 2.30pm, followed by the procession around the village. Four men had to carry the heavy statue and Michele confided that invariably it involved serious discussions behind the scenes as to whose turn it was that year. When Michele, his brother and cousins had the honour of carrying *Sant'Antonio*, he told me afterwards that he had had to pay to be one of the chosen four. Seeing the look of shock-horror on my face, he hastened to add that all proceeds went to the church.

I remember being surprised to see the women leading the procession: one carried a cross and others held huge candles. The statue of *Sant'Antonio* followed them. Two altar servers flanked the priest who recited prayers through a megaphone. A local church band accompanied the marchers, and traffic came to a standstill as we filed along in the middle of the road. Men stood at strategic points with collection bags which they shook at the marchers if ignored.

"Let's go and see what we can get at the *pesca*," Michele had said, giving me a fistful of tickets the first time I'd gone to the festival.

"What's a *pesca*?" I'd never come across the word before other than in the context of fishing.

"It's like – 'ow you say? – I know, a sort of lucky dip," he replied.

I found out that in actual fact, it wasn't really a lucky dip at all. You could buy as many tickets as you liked and then, in the church hall, you handed them over to volunteers who found the objects which were stacked on shelves, each with a corresponding number to the tickets sold outside. Supposedly, you were given your matching number – but – if a child came in with a handful of tickets and an expectant smile, only to have won two pairs of extra-large, thick, black tights, a bar of soap, a headscarf, and an empty biscuit tin, these in turn were switched for suitable items or toys. Obviously, such goings-on sent the well-prepared set-up into utter chaos. The more serious volunteers behind the table were thrown into total panic as numbers mysteriously disappeared and they had to use their initiative by giving a substitute gift and behaving as if everything went according to plan. Now and again, sharp looks were given amongst the helpers, answered by helpless shrugs... all very civilised and all very Italian.

People involved in the festival organised games, weather permitting. One year, someone lent out their guinea pigs for the afternoon's entertainment. Children chose a numbered bucket and if a guinea-pig ran into it, they won a prize. Both Alex and Elisa came home with a prize and a smile. There was also a sack race and a tug of war for the children. A tall tree near the church, provided amusement for the men: they strung a salami high up in the boughs and had to guess the height.

"It's got to be 4 metres at the most."

"What are you talking about? It's not less than 5 metres." The arguing and raised voices were all part of the fun. The winner usually cut it into slices there and then and shared it out with homemade bread which one of the older women baked for the occasion. One of the farmers donated a huge, round cheese which people had to hold and then guess the weight. Again, the winner, if from the parish, put it together with the salami and offered a *spuntino* to anyone who was peckish. However, should the prize go to a Milanese, then the cheese was carefully wrapped up and taken home. Just by looking at the forlorn faces of the contestants who had lost, perhaps only by one ounce or two, you could almost hear such comments as: what a waste of a good cheese!

At 5pm, all activities stopped for the lottery which proved to be a very serious business. The prizes were always good quality, donated mostly by local shops, and the first three consisted of an electrical appliance of some sort, for example, a television or microwave or washing-machine, a coffee table or a dinner service, a set of suitcases or a bicycle.

"Wow," I whispered to Michele. "If you were the winner at my church fete at home, you'd get a bottle of wine and box of chocolates."

"Ssh, it's about to start," he replied as lottery tickets were pulled out of pockets and wallets, reading glasses appeared and a group of young children were chosen to pull the winning numbers out of the bag.

A round of applause followed each prize and the tension grew as the last three numbers were called, then, all too soon, it was over and time to say goodbye. The organisers cleared away and the priest gave them a hand. Comments were made on the amount of money collected and whether more people had turned up this year than the last. We made our way back to Michele's family's house and the conversation during the evening meal was about who we had spoken to, and who had won a lottery prize and how *Zia* Alma had a winning streak because she always won something and Gina had won three prizes and it wasn't really fair to the others... and we didn't see the Barona cousins from Nuova Olonio, wonder why they hadn't come. The more excited they became, the louder they spoke. I still had to get used to the fact that no-one waited for the speaker to finish before replying, but everyone had their say regardless.

*

Over the past twelve years, together with four other women, I've been helping to clean the church on a regular basis and have become a fervent member of the group preparing for the June festival.

"*Sembra un po' sporco,*" Lory said one year, inspecting the statue which had been placed on a table near the altar ready for the following Sunday.

"*E' meglio se lo pulisco.*" And off she went to get a damp cloth.

Looking at the statue more closely, it did seem a bit dusty so while Lory cleaned *Sant' Antonio*, we got on with our chores. All of a sudden, we heard a shout.

"*Oh no, la tunica è diventata rigata,*" Lory said. The rest of us couldn't help laughing as we saw that the brown tunic now sported fashionable stripes at the side.

"*Meno male che abbiamo tempo di metterla a posto,*" she added. "*Sono sicura che ho un po' di pittura marrone a casa.*"

I still had to learn that all good Italian housewives had not only a mini pharmacy at home but also a D.I.Y. kit containing anything and everything. In my case, I was lucky to find a tube of glue and some Sellotape. Half an hour later, Lory had finished painting and we stood back admiring *Sant' Antonio's* make-over. He in turn, looked down on us benevolently, as if to say: *No one will ever know.*

Since my initiation into the circle of helpers, every May, armed with papers from the priest authorising our appeal, I joined Lory and two other women on our quest for lottery and lucky dip prizes. This involved trips to Sondrio, Morbegno and Colico and although I hated the idea of asking for free items, the generosity of the shop owners never failed to amaze me.

On one occasion, my sister, Diane came over the week we'd decided to go to Sondrio and so she joined the party. She watched, fascinated, as we went from shop to shop asking for items for the church festival and couldn't believe how many bags of various articles we accumulated.

"It's incredible," she said. "People are so kind."

"I know, we're really lucky. Our lottery and lucky dip are the best in the area. Everyone talks about the prizes."

The five of us had an ice cream before struggling back to the car with our goods. It usually took us a while to pack everything in the car and it was no different on this particular occasion.

"I never thought you'd get all that in the boot," Diane was suitably impressed.

We settled into the back seat with the remaining bags at our feet and discussed which places we still had to go to in Morbegno. We hadn't gone far before a police car caught up with us. From where I was sitting, I could see them in the wing mirror. Wanting to, they had the chance to overtake us but they didn't. Lory looked in the rear mirror and caught my eye. She looked up again and then checked the speedometer.

"*No, non sto superando il limite di velocità,*" she said, "*Allora, ci stanno davvero inseguendo?*"

"What's the matter?" my sister asked.

"Nothing, it's okay." I tried to put Diane's mind at rest but she sensed that something was wrong.

Twisting round, she saw the *Carabinièri* car at a distance.

"Are they following us?" she demanded.

"Of course not, have they set their flashing blue light in action and waved us down to stop?" I wanted to make light of the matter but at the back of my mind I couldn't help but wonder whether it was a coincidence or not.

"*A Morbegno, giro a sinistra e andiamo a Dolce Forno,*" she said, having noted that the police car had been behind us since leaving Sondrio.

Diane naturally expected a translation so I told her we were going to turn left at Morbegno and go to the *Dolce Forno Bar* for a drink. As we went round the roundabout and took the exit on the left, so did the police car.

"*Ci stanno seguendo sul serio,*" I joked and the others laughed – except Diane who was too busy craning her neck to see who was behind us.

"I have to get the flight home tomorrow," she said when she realised the police were still there. All of a sudden, she had visions of being locked up in a small cell until her case came to trial – and what would her

157

case be? Aiding and abetting the locals collecting for *Sant'Antonio*? She shivered despite the warm May afternoon.

"Don't worry, you will," I assured her, not in the least bit worried. Having lived in the Valtellina for nearly thirty years, I considered myself a veteran where Italian drama was concerned. However, as Lory parked the car and the Italian police stopped directly behind us, we stopped smiling as the seriousness of the situation hit us. One of the uniformed officers walked up to the car door and opened it, while the other stood a short distance away, watching us. Now what was going to happen...and more to the point, how would we explain the contents of the boot and the overflowing bags of brand new articles for the lucky dip and the lottery at our feet?

"*Buongiorno,*" Lory said getting out of the car. "*Ho fatto qualcosa di sbagliato?*"

"*Buongiorno. Patente e libretto, grazie.*" Without answering her question as to whether she'd done something wrong, he asked to see her driving licence and log book and then went to speak to his colleague. We decided to join Lory and with difficulty, we managed to extricate ourselves without revealing the bags and watched in silence as one of the officers made a phone call.

"*Chissà cosa vogliono,*" Milena said. At that moment, we all wanted to know what they wanted.

"*Ma non abbiamo fatto niente di male,*" Anita reasoned, but knowing we hadn't done anything wrong still didn't help.

After what seemed an eternity, the police officer returned the papers to Lory and explained that they were looking for a grey Passat just like hers but the phone call he'd made confirmed that the last letter of the number plate was different.

With a curt: *"Buongiorno"*, the police climbed into their car and drove off. We visibly relaxed.

"Sorry I didn't explain what was happening," I apologised to my white-faced sister.

"I don't need a translation, I need a stiff drink!" Diane whispered as we made our way into the *bar*.

"Chiedi a tua sorella se si è divertita questo pomeriggio e se verrà ancora," Anita asked, but Diane had already got the gist of it and managed a small laugh.

"Yes, I enjoyed it until the episode with the police and no, I don't think I'll be coming with you again. Once is quite enough."

I somehow got the impression that there would be no tearful goodbyes when she left the next day.

25

Grannyland!

After our impromptu holiday in Rome with Dina and Angelo, they asked us if we'd like to go to the Adriatic coast with them the following year. We accepted without hesitating. I still missed the sea terribly and despite Michele's attempts at counteracting my *Baker Moments* by taking me to Lake Como, it couldn't compete with Sandbanks or the Dorset coastline. Our week by the sea was the first of our annual summer holidays together.

To date, Michele and I had only gone for a weekend on the Adriatic coast one April with our friends who had a house in one of the *Lidos* and the weather hadn't been warm enough to actually spend time on the beach or in the water. Instead, we had whizzed along the coastal roads on bikes enjoying the sea air and scenery, visiting places of interest. This time, we booked into a family hotel in Igea Marina in August which faced the Adriatic Sea.

"Wow, we've even got sun-loungers and an umbrella," I said to Michele as we walked over to find our *bagnino* who was in charge of our comfort as well as our safety.

"Ben arrivati, sono Daniele," he smiled as he showed us to our places and told us to ask him if there was anything we needed.

"Ciao, grazie," we answered. Daniele couldn't have been more helpful.

I remembered Michele telling me years ago when we were sitting on the beach at Eastbourne one afternoon that in Italy beaches were private and only small areas of sand were left for any non-paying visitors.

Rows of sun-loungers stretched along the beach under multi coloured umbrellas and the gentle lapping of the waves rolled in from the horizon. Sheer bliss! Each *bagno* had a name and number with a play area for children and a strip of sand cordoned off for bowling to keep the adults amused. While Michele and Angelo competed in friendly bowling tournaments, Dina and I went for long walks in the water, chatting about anything and everything. Then we'd relax on our sun beds and chat some more.

"Cocco bello! Cocco bello!" A shrill voice cut through the air and I jumped inadvertently, wondering what was happening.

A tanned young man came into sight strolling along the sea edge holding a wicker basket laden with slices of coconut, a watchful eye for any customers and a ready wink for bikini-clad females.

"Cocco bello! Cocco bello!" he called out again before disappearing from view.

"In England, they sell ice creams," I told Dina.

"Ah." She didn't seem too impressed: what was ice cream compared to fresh coconut?

Our hotel was a family concern and we couldn't fault the quality of the food or the attentiveness of the staff. However, I have to admit to being fascinated by the behaviour of the guests when it came to the self-service buffet before the waiters served the meal we had previously ordered.

"Look, it's like a race to see who reaches the plates first," I whispered to Michele as an elderly woman deliberately elbowed me out of her way.

Then I watched another spritely pensioner delve into each dish on display.

"Goodness, that woman is never going to eat all that!" I stared blatantly at the amount of food piled onto her plate.

"Maybe she 'as a big appetite," Michele reasoned. "Don't forget we are by the sea."

"Well, that would be my lunch not my starter – sea or no sea."

When the hotel changed hands, we moved farther down the coast to Bellaria where we found another very good hotel and here, Dina had to practice self-control to the full. We all teased her when it came to the dessert trolley. She had an extremely sweet tooth and had great difficulty choosing *just one*. The *Riviera Romagna* is well-known for its characteristic dishes and in this particular place, every week there was a menu based on the specialities of the area with a large selection of mouth-watering desserts.

"Guardate che bontà!" she said, ecstatically.

I taught her the phrase: *Food, glorious food!*

Every morning, we joined a group of keen women on the beach for three quarters of an hour to practise *Ginnastica dolce*. I wouldn't have described all of the exercises as being exactly *gentle* but I enjoyed the challenge and I loved the choice of music. Our young instructor's enthusiasm proved contagious and at the end of the week, we all decided that our bodies had definitely become more toned and tanned. Just before lunch, the girl in charge of the Baby Club, organised the Baby Dance which delighted grannies as well as children, and Dina and I took part, happy in the knowledge that our children and grandchildren couldn't see us. Swaying to the left and to the right in the water, splashing each other as we tried desperately to copy the various actions, we laughed and giggled our way through the songs. Most evenings there was some sort of entertainment in the hotel but the four of us preferred to go for a walk into town to see the market stalls and watch the street entertainers.

After a week of relaxing in the warm sun under a crystal blue sky, we came home happy and ready to work. I prepared English lessons for my ever increasing number of students and became more familiar with modern technology. I tried teaching English to Dina but if it didn't have anything to do with the Beatles, she forgot it immediately.

*

When my aunt and her friend went to Lake Garda for a week, I suggested driving down to see them.

"Do you want to come with me?" I asked Michele.

"I would, certainly but I 'ave to work."

"I know, I'll ask Dina. She'll come."

She readily accepted the invitation as she'd never been there before and like me, was excited at the prospect of a day trip. We discussed the route suggested by Google Maps and printed off the directions – how I had managed to function without a pc and the Internet up till now I'll never know – and we ignored the general reaction from the family and friends.

"Won't you get lost?"

"Will you be alright driving on the motorway?"

I reminded them that I'd been doing airport runs for years, including English airports, and had driven various members of the family to Switzerland and back.

We had a smooth journey and Dina proved to be an excellent navigator and typical backseat driver. She made sure I kept my eyes on the road.

"Watch out! There's a lorry in front."

"Yes, I know." I had trouble keeping a straight face. No way could I not see the juggernaut.

"I'll overtake if you like."

"*Sì, sì.* Ah, now I can see the motorway signs. We turn off at the next junction."

We had no problem finding Malcesine and the hotel where my aunt and her friend were staying and we thoroughly enjoyed our day in Lake Garda.

*

I loved my role as *Granny* and naturally, I spoke English to Giulia and Fabio, which caused a few raised eyebrows but I was more than used to it by now, and although my grandchildren, when younger, answered in Italian, they understood everything I said. If anything, as the years slid by, I was busier than ever and when my family came over to visit, they invariably met some of the students either at the house or when we went out and about.

It would have been impossible to get bored teaching because I had a varied assortment of students: some still went to school, others worked and needed English for their job, and then there were retired people who wanted to learn the English language for their holidays abroad. Several students are unforgettable for different reasons: one attractive woman in her twenties invariably got the day wrong – sometimes she came for a lesson a day early and other times a day late. Once she walked in and said:

"Is Elisa here? I think I need a Shiatsu massage more than an English lesson this evening."

That said, she forfeited her time with me learning the finer points of the *Present Perfect* tense for an hour of concentrated pummelling on her meridian points, feeling much better and less stressed when she left.

A group of pensioners impressed me by their tenacity to learn enough English to go to Amsterdam on their own. They came back euphoric to think they had understood everything and had been understood.

I nicknamed one group of two sisters and their friend who were at senior school, the *Singing Trio* because they used to make up a song and sing it to me at the end of each school term. When they went to university, they still came to see me. Occasionally, I taught the son or daughter of one of my early pupils. I watched unsure adolescents blossom into mature adults and most of them kept in touch, popping in to see me at Christmas often with a present.

"Honestly," Mum used to say, "they pay for lessons and give you presents, too. It could only happen in Italy."

26

Where are my Sleeves?

Opening the shutters one morning and looking out onto the snow-capped mountains, I had to admit that life was good. Now and again, I received a phone call from the CTP, a school at Delebio, a small town on the opposite side of the river Adda from Piussogno, asking if I'd be interested in taking evening classes but I always declined because with choir practice and other commitments, I had a fairly full schedule.

We also had Elisa's wedding to look forward to in May. Whereas *San Michele* will always be attributed to Alex and Lorena's wedding, *Sant'Antonio* will always remind me of Elisa and Cristian's because they told us they were going to get married the following year, when we came home after the festivities.

*

"Mum, can you believe it, my wedding dress has arrived but not the sleeves and they won't be here before the first week of May!" A slight tremble in her voice betrayed my daughter's normally positive attitude to life, but what could I say? She had chosen a dress from a shop which liaised with one in America where the dresses were actually made, and although it had seemed like a good idea at the time, now it looked like a monster of a hiccup.

"Listen, the wedding is nearly a month away, so we've got plenty of time." I did my best to sound reassuring but in actual fact I couldn't help worrying. Her detachable sleeves were an intrinsic part of the dress and without them I envisaged more than a headache for us.

"Let's have a cup of tea," I suggested.

"Mum, I don't want a cup of tea, I want my sleeves!"

Our son, Alex and Lorena had arranged their wedding in six months, nine years ago and, apart from a few hitches regarding the restructuring of their flat, everything had gone smoothly. Naturally, I expected this one to be no different.

"Mum, I want the roses for my bouquet to be this colour," my daughter said, holding up a tiny fuchsia rosebud. Elisa certainly knew what she wanted. She scoured the florists relentlessly until she found the exact coloured roses for her bouquet and then asked me for my opinion regarding the flower arrangements she'd selected for the church.

"Mum, will you come with me to look for a wedding dress?"

Would I? I'd been waiting years for this moment.

"Of course I will!"

Seeing my daughter standing before me in a mass of white satin with a bodice of French lace left me speechless, an event in itself. However, two weeks later, having tried on numerous different styles and looking through brochures in three bridal shops, Elisa still hadn't found what she was looking for.

"Oh well, there are lots more shops to go to." Or so I thought.

Eventually, she found the dress of her dreams and Michele and I accompanied her for the fitting. Our daughter looked lovely. Fortunately, the elusive sleeves found their way across the Atlantic in good time, and all was fine until the day we went to collect the dress.

"*Papà*, stop the car! I can't remember if the veil is in the bag or not."

Michele parked as soon as possible and Elisa jumped out to check the bag in the boot.

"Nooo!" We didn't need to ask any questions. Her wedding dress, shoes and other accessories were packed in the car – but not her veil. Retracing our way back to the shop, I realised a near disaster had just been avoided. The shop was not only a good half an hour away from Piussogno by car but it was only open by appointment.

*

My family and friends came from England for the wedding and Alex and Lorena took over the catering side, realising that maybe it wouldn't be a good idea for me to feed a minimum of twenty-three people at each sitting over several days. The evening before the wedding, a group of friends, led by the groom-to-be, came to serenade Elisa. With the help of a constant flowing jug of red wine, the singers filled the still night air with words that came from the heart. We all agreed – it was pure magic.

Despite the previous dull, wet weekends, a bright blue sky and brilliant sunshine heralded the day of the wedding

"Mum, where are they? They should be here by now!" For a moment my daughter, usually so calm and collected, was in panic mode.

"Don't worry! They'll be here any minute." Crossing my fingers, I willed her best friends to walk through the front door. They didn't, of course, and Elisa looked once more out of the window, then at her wedding dress hidden inside an elaborate white cover, before pacing the bedroom floor.

"You won't forget to take my comfy shoes, will you?"

"No!"

"And you won't…" Her sentence went unfinished as a shrill ringing of the doorbell announced the arrival of her two friends and laughing and giggling like fifteen year olds, they disappeared into her room to dress the bride. 'Yes,' I thought to myself, 'Saturday, 22nd May, 2010 will certainly be a date to remember in the Baker/ Barona household.'

I checked my watch: 1.30pm, people would soon be arriving and I still hadn't changed. With 230 guests, this promised to be some wedding.

"Why aren't you dressed? Everyone's 'ere already!" Michele, the father of the bride, took his role very seriously in typical Italian style. He had been organising the buffet for the past two months and had bought enough food and drink for the entire population of our village.

"Valerie Anne, get in that bedroom and change into your wedding outfit!" My mum, a sprightly octogenarian, dared me to do otherwise.

"Give me five minutes." Closing the door, I thought back to my own wedding which had been organised in three months – and by my mum, no less. A lot had happened since I first arrived in Piussogno, in 1977... And now Michele would soon accompany our daughter up the aisle. Where had the years gone? Before I lost myself in reveries, I changed in record time and joined the guests.

27

The Choir Goes To London

"You know, it would be lovely to take the choir to London to see the sights and go to organ recitals and hear the choir in St Paul's Cathedral," Patrizia said, wistfully.

"Let's go then." I was always ready to go to England.

"We'll see what they say after the next choir practice," she decided.

Patrizia went to London regularly at the end of each school year and so we suggested organising a long weekend while she was there. There was mixed reaction from the choir members: some, like me, were ready to go, others wanted to know more before committing themselves, and a few said they didn't want to go. Nearly all of them said it was far too early to start planning – Italians hardly ever make arrangements so long in advance – but we both knew that it would take a lot of time and effort to organise the trip in July and nine months wasn't too soon.

While teaching at a local pre-school, taking choir practices and looking after her family, Patrizia still managed to make all the necessary arrangements. She booked us into the place near the Oval where she stayed each year. She went to a travel agency in Morbegno and booked seventeen seats on an early flight and then she organised a fun-packed itinerary including sightseeing, an organ recital and service in St Paul's Cathedral. An air of expectation permeated through Piussogno and as the departure date drew nearer the excited participants wanted to know how we were getting to the airport. Not wanting to risk going to Malpensa Airport in individual cars with the possibility of a flat tyre or even worse, an accident and missing our flight, we decided to hire a minibus.

Patrizia and I had both emphasised the fact that the group needed to take an umbrella because the English weather could be so unpredictable but for once, the sun shone in a clear blue sky and we didn't even need a jumper. We stayed in a hostel run by Maltese nuns and on our arrival, I had a terrible urge to laugh when the one in charge repeated a set of rules as she handed out the keys as if we were school girls. I nicknamed our room *the cell* and Tunella, my *cell mate*, and I irreverently added a few more regulations to the list.

Making sure seventeen Italians all managed to get on the same tube or bus became a challenge but not a physical impossibility – Patrizia and I switched into teacher mode. Only once did a group get left behind and Patrizia had to jump off at the next station – having gestured frantically to them to wait where they were – and go back to get them while I stayed with the others on the tube and got off at our arranged destination. It was all part of the fun.

"Cosa vuol dire 'sorree'?" Tunella asked me, after a passer-by had said it to one of our group.

"Sorry means *'scusa'*.

They had plenty of practice when they accidently bumped into someone on the tube, on the bus or on the crowded pavements.

"How could you leave all this?" they asked me, lapsing into dialect, as we gazed out of the Millennium Eye, mesmerised by spectacular views of the city.

"Don't forget I come from Poole, not London," I reminded them.

"Yes, but your town is near the capital, isn't it?" someone else said.

"Well, it isn't exactly down the road," I tried to explain, "I suppose it's about the same distance from Piussogno to Milan. London is very special, though...and so is Poole."

"And you gave all this up for Michele," another choir member added.

"Yes, I did." I'd certainly have a lot to tell Michele when I rang him that evening.

"You must have been very homesick when you came to Piussogno, leaving all this."

"I can't say it was easy at the time but now I'm quite happy where I am," I answered truthfully.

"Oh look! There's a double decker bus..." You could almost feel their excitement.

Apart from comments regarding English gastronomy, everyone enthused over the sightseeing tour Patrizia gave the group. Watching them pointing to a monument or taking a photo of the Thames, I couldn't help but wonder at the difference between life in Piussogno and life in a city. I suddenly realised that, having lived for so long in Italy, I felt more like a tourist than a native and Patrizia was far more familiar with London than me.

The Sunday service in St Paul's enthralled our group and became the highlight of our trip. As we filed out of the cathedral, no one wanted to leave, so we decided to have an impromptu picnic in the church grounds. While Milena delved into her haversack to find salami, cheese and a bottle of wine, two others went in search of bread and I paired up with Claudia to buy fruit. Naturally, someone had remembered to ask a nun for a knife to slice the salami and cheese – Italians are so incredibly organised where food is concerned. It was only after our meal that we realised that what had served as a table was actually a tomb. Still, not many choirs in northern Italy can boast of having sung in St Paul's, then had lunch outside in the cathedral grounds.

28

Full Circle

An infernally hot summer came and went and in September, I had yet another call from the CTP at Delebio, asking if I was interested in giving English conversation and this time, after much deliberation, I accepted.

"Mi puoi dire cosa significa CTP, per favore?" I realised I had no idea what the letters stood for.

"Certo. Centro Territoriale Permanente."

The secretary then explained that the Life Long Learning Centre was a school which catered for adult education, specifically Italian courses, and also offered foreign language and computer ones. Apparently, a number of people had enquired about English conversation lessons.

It meant giving up my place in the choir because I'd now be teaching instead of singing but I really missed being in a classroom and knew the time was right for a complete change.

"They asked me to submit a CV and my teaching certificate. At last someone actually wants to see my teaching credentials," I told Michele.

Walking into the building for the first time, I felt as if I'd come full circle. I'd left Poole as a young teacher, eager to put my college years into practice but since arriving in Piussogno, I had never had the opportunity to teach for more than a few months at a time. Now I had the chance to do the job I loved on a permanent basis.

Monica, who was head of the foreign languages department, introduced herself and couldn't have been more helpful. She also introduced me to Cinzia, who as well as being the head of the Italian department, acted as a *referente* or contact person; her dynamic personality reflected the contents of her personal cupboard which proved to be more like Aladdin's Cave than a typical classroom one.

"There's everything you can think of in here from books and the usual school paraphernalia to food, comfortable shoes and slippers but there are two fundamental things you'll never find: men or money!" Cinzia told me, laughing.

Monica showed me her more sober cupboard containing the English material she had compiled over the years and pointed out the shelf where she kept books and visual aids necessary for my lessons and then I met the other members of the staff who all made me feel very welcome. I waited impatiently for my first class and loved every minute of it; the students were enthusiastic and responded actively and imaginatively to the topics I prepared. Over the months, the groups increased and then Monica asked if I'd take a Beginners course. This proved to be a challenge for me as well as the students because being used to conducting my lessons in English, the Italians hadn't the faintest idea what I was talking about and I found sixteen pairs of extremely wide eyes looking at me out of stricken faces. However, after a chat with Monica, I adapted my method of teaching to their requirements and with the help of visual aids and a certain amount of Italian incorporated into the lessons, we came to a happy compromise.

"'Ow did it go?" Michele asked as I put my bag on the table after finishing the lesson before the Christmas holidays.

"Brilliantly," I told him. "One of the students brought a *Tiramisù* she'd made – which was absolutely delicious – and others brought cold drinks and a bottle of sparkling wine."

"Cosa?" he could hardly believe his ears.

"Yes, and we said she'll have to make another one at the end of the school year."

So began my career on the staff at evening school between enjoyable lessons, mouth-watering plates of *Tiramisù* and impromptu birthday parties complete with presents.

However, it wasn't only the number of students that was increasing, on the home front, my family continued to grow with the arrival of Elisa and Cristian's son, Paolo in 2011. Two years later, their daughter Lucia was born in May, and Elena, Alex and Lorena's daughter, arrived five months later in October. 2013 can only be described as being extremely exciting and fruitful.

*

"Anything special happening from 10th to 12th May next year?" I asked the family who had come for one of my inimitable lasagnes.

"Why, are you going somewhere?" Alex looked up from his plate.

"Yes, I am. I'm going to Dublin with the English group at the CTP."

Silence reigned as they digested this piece of information. It was a typically grey, autumnal evening and apart from the arrival of our new granddaughter, Elena, there had been no surprises lately.

"Lucia will be one on Thursday, 8th May but is there anything else that I've forgotten like Christenings or First Communions?"

Before I actually confirmed a place on Monica's list I wanted to be sure I wouldn't be missing out on any major family events. With five grandchildren to date, teaching commitments, village events, not to mention trips to see my family in England, you could say I was quite busy.

"We'll probably celebrate Lucia's birthday with cousins at the weekend but we can have a party for grandparents on the eighth," said Elisa.

"I don't think there's anything at the moment," Alex replied. "But it's a bit early to plan ahead, isn't it?"

"Yes, it is – by Italian standards," I couldn't help adding. "Do you want to come with me?" I asked Michele. "You'll have to enrol on one of the English classes with me or if you'd rather, you can go with Monica."

His look said it all and I gathered I'd be going alone. I didn't mind, though. I'd be back before he had time to miss me. I'd always wanted to visit Dublin and now, thanks to the school, I could. Monica had the difficult job of organising our weekend in Ireland and naturally, she didn't want to leave anything to chance. I just had to write a couple of emails and check her itinerary. Although our trip was seven months away, I knew the time would fly by – and it did.

"Quando parti, Nonna?" asked Fabio, my eight year old grandson.

"I'm going to Dublin next weekend," I answered.

"E quanti siete?" He was certainly one for detail.

"Twenty-nine of us: twenty-four students, four teachers and the head teacher."

"Beh, speriamo che non vi perdete," he said.

"Yes, I hope we don't get lost, too," I agreed.

Although my main worry was another. When speaking to Italians, even those who I didn't know, I had a habit of forgetting to use the formal *'lei'*, especially if they were good company and about my age. On hearing that the head teacher would be one of the group, I knew I'd have to be extremely careful not to lapse into the informal manner of speaking. However, the evening before our flight, I had something even more important to think about. Checking the weather forecast before choosing what clothes to put in my hand-luggage, I saw that temperatures in Dublin were somewhat lower than the ones in northern Italy. After much debate and a quick phone call to my sister in Winterborne Kingston, I decided to take my winter jacket – just in case – and was I glad. Gale force winds and cold rain met us off the plane at Dublin Airport the following afternoon.

A coach took us to our hotel and after freshening-up, we donned our coats and braved the elements to visit the town. Showers stopped as quickly as they started and we all commented on the marvellous rainbows that appeared. Our first stop on our sightseeing tour was the Bank of Ireland which had originally been the Irish Parliament.

"*Perchè non ci sono le finestre?*" a student asked.

"That's a good question. I looked it up on the Internet but couldn't find an explanation for it not having any windows." I thought for a moment and then added, "perhaps glass cost too much at the time of building."

Another student, who hadn't heard what I'd said, repeated more or less the same thing so I deducted that the theory had a feasible ring to it. Even so, it bugged me to think I hadn't been able to give them an answer. Italians, by nature, want to know the reason behind a fact and a simple *perhaps* to their *why* just isn't appropriate – as I'd found out during my first course with the Beginners Group. English lessons went well until we had to study the past tense and I introduced irregular verbs.

"*Perchè alcuni verbi sono regolari e altri sono irregolari?*" a student asked me.

"Well, because some are regular and some are irregular," I said, helplessly wondering who had invented the list of verbs in the first place.

"*Come facciamo a sapere quali sono regolari e quali no?*" asked another.

"There's no rule. You just have to learn the list of irregular verbs," I explained to a sea of accusing faces.

"Sorry," I added, hoping that an apology might alleviate the situation. It didn't. The fact that there are no rules for certain grammar points in the English language left me feeling very inadequate and I couldn't help saying:

"Well, what do you expect? We drive on the left side of the road..."

With all this in mind, I vowed to find out the reason for the Bank of Ireland being windowless.

The statue of Molly Malone was next on our itinerary but holding an umbrella while checking the road map flapping uncontrollably under the effect of impromptu gusts proved a feat in itself. In the end, we resorted to verbal directions and asked a friendly Dubliner who offered to take us there. As we walked along the rain drenched streets, I asked him if he knew the reason why the Bank of Ireland had no windows. He stopped in his tracks, scratched his head then shook it.

"Do you know something? I'm a Dubliner and I've lived here all my life but I don't know why there are no windows in the building. I never thought about it before. Can you believe it?"

"Cos'ha detto?" asked an attentive student who had understood my question but had missed the answer.

"He doesn't know why there are no windows in the Bank of Ireland," I said, somewhat smugly. If a native couldn't tell us, I didn't feel quite so inadequate. I changed the subject and like all true Brits, decided to talk about the weather – the climate in Dublin seemed a lot cooler and damper than Poole.

Unfortunately, when we arrived in Grafton Street, all we found was a wet, grey slab where the statue should have been and a local policeman explained that it had been removed a few days earlier for maintenance work. Instead of immortalising the infamous fishmonger with her cart, we took a group photo with the kindly Irishman and then Monica explained Molly Malone's story. Standing on the exact spot where her statue had been, Monica sang the famous Molly Malone song and I followed with an Anglo rendering of 'Cockles and Mussels'! It caused quite an attraction and I was sorry not to have had a hat to pass around the crowd…

Strolling through the famous Temple Bar area gave us a glimpse of Dublin by night. Street entertainers offered typical Irish music, Dubliners dressed up as Leprechauns allowed themselves to be photographed – for a price, and human statues beckoned to anyone who looked their way. The smell of freshly cooked dishes filled our nostrils and dividing into groups, we decided to find somewhere to eat.

"Venite, venite! Abbiamo trovato un posto!" one of the students shouted to us. The head teacher had found a pub large enough to accommodate 29 hungry Italians. While Monica translated for the group upstairs, I looked after the students downstairs in a dimly lit area which gave the impression of serving as a night club. An extremely helpful young Irish waiter distributed menus and cutlery and whispered several phrases which,

unfortunately, I couldn't understand. His Dublin accent foiled me completely but too proud to admit it to the group, I improvised.

"Che cos'ha detto?" they asked me.

"The waiter wants to take your orders and I offered to help him," I said, crossing my fingers.

As we were finishing our fish and chips and Irish stew, the waiter appeared and once again he said something I just didn't understand. As soon as he left, I announced that he'd come to check that all was well and a general muttering of how kind he was filled the room. The next time he came downstairs, I could tell he had a problem and trying very hard to decipher what he said, all was revealed. The place we had taken over had been booked for 10pm for a hen party with a male stripper. I quickly explained the situation to the group and muffled a laugh when some asked if they could stay. The waiter interpreted their query correctly and said it was by invitation only. We left as quietly as Italians could.

Walking back to our hotel, I found myself together with the head teacher as well as my travelling companion, Ilaria. The continual showers couldn't dampen our lively conversation and we arrived back at our hotel in no time.

The next morning, I enjoyed watching the reactions as several Italians tried the full Irish fried breakfast. They gingerly inspected the black pudding before smelling it then prodded the white pudding.

"Why don't you eat a fried breakfast?" asked a student sitting opposite me.

Tucking into my cereal I told her that my bacon-and-egg days were over.

"I always used to when I went to school but now I prefer a lighter breakfast."

"Ah, you want to be thin not fat," another student quipped.

"Good! You remember your adjectives," I was suitably impressed.

Half an hour later, we set off for St Patrick's Cathedral and I had the challenge of speaking Italian and translating simultaneously making as few mistakes as possible. The young guide inside the church was very helpful and showed us where to find Jonathan Swift's tomb. On a whim, I asked her if she knew why the Bank of Ireland had no windows.

"Yes, I can tell you," she said. "It's because the government put a tax on glass and it was too expensive so they built it without any windows."

"Great! Thank you very much." Now I could put the record straight and both the Italians and I would be happy.

No one can visit Dublin without going to the Guinness Store. However, several members of our group chose to do something else so we went our separate ways. Once again, I found myself with the head teacher and Ilaria and together we pulled our first pint of Guinness. Not having a penchant for any type of beer, I gave my perfect glass to another Italian who accepted it gratefully and downed it as if it were water.

We spent a while at the top of the building, literally drinking in the spectacular views from the glass dome of

Dublin. The students lapsed naturally into their mother tongue and as the Guinness kicked in, the volume rose slightly as they enthused over the panorama.

"E' ora di pranzo," one of the group announced, as we trooped out of the store and the others agreed that lunch was a good idea.

Despite the cold weather and unpredictable showers, we managed to see everything on our itinerary, even fitting in a train ride to a picturesque fishing village where we stopped for a succulent evening meal of fish and chips finishing off with an Irish coffee. What more could we want!

Epilogue

After living nearly forty years in Italy, I have obviously become a native. I can proudly say I drive like an Italian, gesticulate like an Italian, discuss football like an Italian and – even though it's taken years – I try and cook like an Italian. Sometimes I get irritated when I go shopping and find a *Back Soon!* sign on the shop door and sometimes I wish the shops didn't close for lunch and a siesta, but now I tend to accept it; I also have the choice of going to the shopping centre where the shops are open all day if I want to.

I often have a craving for sausages and baked beans, bacon butties, gravy, apple crumble and custard but thanks to Julie and Gino, who opened their very own multi-ethnic restaurant recently, I can treat myself to Fish and Chips with Sarson's malt vinegar whenever I feel like it. After twenty-five years, my weekly coffee mornings in Morbegno with Julie are still sacred, giving each other support and advice when needed, together with a lot of laughter.

My family in England would probably say I also speak like an Italian, too – the usual *'sì, sì'* becomes 'yes, yes'. Occasionally, I *Italianise* an English word and vice versa but when I'm in teacher mode, I sincerely hope that nobody can fault my grammar. I enjoy working at the CTP, which has now become the CPIA (*Centro Provinciale Istruzione Adulti* or Life Long Learning Centre for the County of Sondrio), with a new head teacher – who also speaks a little English! Cinzia has been promoted to deputy head and is busier than ever. I asked her once if she actually went home to sleep or whether she had a bed hidden away in a corner. Monica is still responsible for foreign languages and helps out with Italian classes, too. Both of them work tirelessly but with a smile, their enthusiasm and professionalism inevitably rubbing off on whoever they meet.

While chatting to them after our lessons, Monica confided to me recently that she has always wanted to write a grammar book for English students, which explains the reason for her cabinet bursting with reams of photocopies just waiting to be put to good use, and asked me if I would be willing to work on the project. With that in mind, neither of us will be retiring for a very long time. Finding myself on the staff and teaching in a classroom on a regular basis, albeit evening classes, is like a dream come true.

Michele is still working – even though he'd rather be retired – especially on cold, dark winter mornings when he has to get up and I'm snuggled beneath the duvet. Just for a change, his favourite football team, *Fiorentina* is causing him grief this season; the players aren't performing as well as expected. However, when they manage to win a match, everyone in the Barona household is happy – at least until the next game.

Michele and I are very lucky to have two great children who have given us five grandchildren to date – one never knows if anymore will come along in the future... and *Villa Barona* is almost always full of *little people* shouting and singing at different decibels. Playing with the grandchildren keeps us young and if I find it increasingly difficult to sit cross-legged under the table, I'm not going to tell anyone – yet.

The majestic mountains encircling us, which I once found so stifling and ominous, have since become a gentle green palisade, and when I venture out of the Valtellina, I actually find myself missing them. I don't miss the English beaches so much since our family summer holidays on the Adriatic coast, and last but not least, *Baker Moments* are extremely rare these days – probably due to my fairly hectic schedule. I came from Poole to Piussogno a lifetime ago, unsure as to whether I'd ever be able to adapt fully to village ways – but, quite honestly, now I could never move away from my adopted home and our family and friends. In fact, life couldn't be better!

Acknowledgments

Firstly, a big thank you to my family for their ongoing support, especially when I'd disappear into my study at the wrong time – invariably when I'd invited everyone for a meal – because I'd suddenly have a brainwave and *just had to write it down*.

Heartfelt thanks to my son, Alex and daughter, Elisa who had the job of vetting the book. They also played an important part in helping me find the exact photo for the book cover when they suggested going out for an ice cream one afternoon.

A big thank you also goes to my daughter-in-law, Lorena who checked the Italian dialogue for me.

I'd like to thank my aunt, Eileen Burton for her advice on various aspects of the book.

Special thanks to my sister-in-law, Debbie Baker who gave me helpful suggestions where needed.

Thanks also to my brother-in-law, Gordon Kerr who answered my last-minute queries, giving sound advice and helpful hints.

Special thanks go to Kathy Stallard who was my number one critic, making the appropriate corrections when needed. Many thanks, also to her husband, Colin for his help with technicalities regarding the chapter on microlighting.

Thanks to Ivan Guglielmana who gave helpful suggestions with the chapter describing my claim to fame as a Hardcore singer and more importantly, coming to the rescue when my *'techno'* abilities failed me and I couldn't make the cover photos for the book exactly as I wanted them.

Thanks to my loyal friend, Julie Schindler for her unfailing support and talking me through imaginary literary problems while sipping cups of coffee in our favourite *bar* in Morbegno.

I'd like to thank everyone who gave subtle hints and ideas when *writer's block* set in with a vengeance.

And lastly, a huge thank you to my husband, Michele for waiting patiently for his meals, knowing that sooner or later, something would appear on the table! Thanks to him, my children and grandchildren, the true significance of *Mamma Mia… That's Life!* comes to the fore – the family.

A Christmas Baby
for the Cowboy

A Christmas Baby for the Cowboy

A Careys of Cowboy Point Novel

Megan Crane

TULE
PUBLISHING